LONGMAN LITERATURE

The Devil's Disciple

Bernard Shaw

Editor: Ian Wilson

LONGMAN

Longman Literature
Series editor: Roy Blatchford

Plays

Alan Ayckbourn **Absurd Person Singular** 0 582 06020 6
Ad de Bont **Mirad, A Boy from Bosnia** 0 582 24949 X
Oliver Goldsmith **She Stoops to Conquer** 0 582 25397 7
Henrik Ibsen **Three plays: The Wild Duck, Ghosts and A Doll's House** 0 582 24948 1
Ben Jonson **Volpone** 0 582 25408 6
Christopher Marlowe **Doctor Faustus** 0 582 25409 4
Arthur Miller **An Enemy of the People** 0 582 09717 7
Terence Rattigan **The Winslow Boy** 0 582 06019 2
Jack Rosenthal **Wide-Eyed and Legless** 0 582 24950 3
Willy Russell **Educating Rita** 0 582 06013 3
  Shirley Valentine 0 582 08173 4
Peter Shaffer **Equus** 0 582 09712 6
  The Royal Hunt of the Sun 0 582 06014 1
Bernard Shaw **Arms and the Man** 0 582 07785 0
  The Devil's Disciple 0 582 25410 8
  Pygmalion 0 582 06015 X
  Saint Joan 0 582 07786 9
R B Sheridan **The Rivals** and **The School for Scandal** 0 582 25396 9
J Webster **The Duchess of Malfi** 0 582 28731 6
Oscar Wilde **The Importance of Being Earnest** 0 582 07784 2

Longman Literature Shakespeare
Series editor: Roy Blatchford

A Midsummer Night's Dream 0 582 08833 X (paper)
  0 582 24590 7 (cased)
Antony and Cleopatra 0 582 28727 8 (paper)
As You Like It 0 582 23661 4 (paper)
Coriolanus 0 582 28726 X
Hamlet 0 582 09720 7 (paper)
Henry IV Part I 0 582 23660 6 (paper)
Henry V 0 582 22584 1 (paper)
Julius Caesar 0 582 08828 3 (paper)
  0 582 24589 3 (cased)
King Lear 0 582 09718 5 (paper)
Macbeth 0 582 08827 5 (paper)
  0 582 24592 3 (cased)
The Merchant of Venice 0 582 08835 6 (paper)
  0 582 24593 1 (cased)
Othello 0 582 09719 3 (paper)
Richard III 0 582 23663 0 (paper)
Romeo and Juliet 0 582 08836 4 (paper)
  0 582 24591 5 (cased)
The Tempest 0 582 22583 3 (paper)
Twelfth Night 0 582 08834 8 (paper)
The Winter's Tale 0 582 28727 8

Other titles in the Longman Literature series are listed on page 123

Contents

CONTENTS

The writer on writing

Shaw's life

George Bernard Shaw (1856–1950) was born in Dublin to unhappily married parents. His father was a drunkard and his mother neglected her children, leaving their care to servants. He went to several schools where he learnt little and left early. In 1871 he started work as a clerk, and left after four years, moving to London in 1876. During the next decade he struggled to become a writer, selling occasional brief reviews and a few articles to the papers, with no author's name attached. These were mostly on musical events or subjects.

He also wrote five novels at this time, but at first he could not get them published. His sixth attempt, **An Unsocial Socialist**, was finally published (in instalments) in 1884, followed over the next four years by three of the previous novels. Shaw later worked as a critic, writing on the theatre, art, and most notably music (using the pseudonym Corno di Bassetto, the Italian for 'basset horn'). His interest in political questions was stimulated by his reading of Marx, and he became a socialist. In 1884 he joined the recently founded Fabian Society which aimed to bring about socialism in Britain by peaceful means, and he became one of its most effective propagandists.

Shaw was greatly influenced by the Norwegian playwright Henrik Ibsen. Ibsen took social themes, treated them realistically, and condemned above all the crushing effects of society and its conventions upon the human personality. Shaw's first play, **Widowers' Houses** was begun in 1884, but not produced until 1892. It was followed in rapid succession by **The Philanderer**, **Mrs Warren's Profession**, **Arms and the Man**, **Candida**, and **You Never Can Tell**. All six plays were published together in 1898 as **Plays Pleasant and Unpleasant**. Shaw continued through another fifty plays to use his wit and 'moral passion' to attack injustice, hypocrisy and self-interest.

Shaw was a prodigious writer, and he produced many articles and pamphlets as well as works such as **Common Sense about the War** (1914), **The Intelligent Woman's Guide to Socialism and Capitalism** (1928), and **Everybody's Political What's What?** (1944). He was a constant letter writer, a formidable orator, and also a regular broadcaster.

One of the many problems in considering Shaw as a writer is that he often used his mischievous sense of humour to conceal his real intentions or feelings. He was besieged by journalists, politicians, and members of the public, all demanding to know his opinions on every conceivable subject, and he frequently resorted to hiding behind the personality of 'GBS': irascible, amusing and cynical by turns. He often complained that his persona had been manufactured by the press and public, but it could be argued that he himself contributed almost as much to it: 'The remedy...is sedulous advertisement. Accordingly, I have advertized myself so well that I find myself, whilst still in middle life, almost as legendary a person as the Flying Dutchman' (Preface to **The Devil's Disciple**).

Shaw, despite the evidence of his early struggle to get published, always claimed he found it easy to write:

> I never felt inclined to write, any more than to breathe. It never occurred to me that my literary sense was exceptional: I gave everyone credit for it; for there is nothing miraculous in a natural faculty to the man who has it. In art the amateur, the collector, the enthusiast, is the man who lacks the faculty for producing it. The Venetian wants to be a cavalry soldier; the Gaucho wants to be a sailor, the fish wants to fly and the bird to swim. I never wanted to write. I know now, of course, the scarcity of literary faculty; but I still dont (sic) want it. You cannot want a thing and have it, too.
>
> **Sixteen Self Sketches**, 1949

He also claimed that writing plays had been one of his aims from an early age: 'I write plays because I like it and because I cannot remember any period in my life when I could help inventing people and scenes.'

Shaw's views and his audience

Shaw is often accused of writing his plays simply as propaganda for his political and social views. Before this time, plays were not generally regarded as publishable, but Shaw resolved to make them so by adding readable, novelistic stage directions. In addition, he wrote prefaces for most of the plays, in which he explained the ideas which he hoped to promote. Sometimes these prefaces, which can be almost as long as the plays themselves, were used to attack critics of his work or to promote theories only vaguely related to the themes of the plays. Certainly, Shaw felt that 'serious drama is perhaps the most formidable social weapon that a modern reformer can wield' (Michael Holroyd, **Bernard Shaw**, vol. 1).

Between 1895 and 1898, Shaw worked as the drama critic for a weekly magazine, **Saturday Review**, and was still writing for it while composing **The Devil's Disciple**. The magazine was a small-circulation paper, edited by Frank Harris (who later wrote a life of Shaw), but Shaw was delighted to have a platform for his views on drama. He had written five plays by this time, but only two had been put on commercially, and Shaw was, understandably, hostile to the West End theatre of the day. This relied heavily on costly productions of plays which made no demands at all on the intellects of those who flocked to see them. The plays were often very crude or silly, but drew large crowds of pleasure-seekers.

There was, however, an alternative to the West End. A few independent producers tried to break away from the stifling predictability of the commercial theatre. They often had to use theatre clubs rather than public theatres because of the need to escape the attentions of the censor, the Lord Chamberlain. (These duties of the Lord Chamberlain were not abolished until the 1960s.) Shaw championed this new drama in his criticism, but he was sensible enough to realise that it was useless to call for popular entertainment to be replaced by the works of Ibsen and the like. In politics, as a Fabian, Shaw argued for the infiltration of the existing structures of power by people with socialist beliefs. Similarly he argued for the need to persuade the more imaginative managers to incorporate more serious works into their seasons of farce and melodrama. Shaw to some extent, adopted a version of this strategy in writing his plays. The plot of **Mrs Warren's Profession** is borrowed from a successful West End play by Pinero, **The Second Mrs Tanqueray**; **You Never Can Tell** is a farce; and **The Devil's Disciple** is an old-fashioned melodrama. Shaw realised that he had to use these forms of play if there was to be any chance of his work being put on by the commercial theatre: 'dividing form from content, he valued such work by how skilfully it permeated the commercial theatre with social and artistic truth' (Michael Holroyd, **Bernard Shaw**, vol. 1). Even while recognising this necessity, Shaw could still pretend to be above it all: 'Some plays are written to please the author; some to please the actor-manager (these are the worst); some to please the public; and some – my own, for instance – to please nobody' (**Saturday Review**, 16 October 1897).

Looking back over his career as a dramatist, when writing the Preface to **Back to Methuselah** in 1921, Shaw observed:

> In my own activities as a playwright … I tried slum-landlordism, doctrinaire Free Love, prostitution, militarism, marriage, history, current politics, natural Christianity, national and individual character, paradoxes of conventional society, husband-hunting, questions of conscience, professional delusions and impostures, all worked into a series of comedies of manners in the classic fashion.

Some critics have taken the view that Shaw's characters in the early plays can be one-dimensional, lacking the emotions and contradictory feelings of adults. One can admire the craftsmanship of Shaw's writing, the way in which he took the forms of drama which Victorian audiences were used to and twisted them for his own ends; but one always has to remember Shaw's purpose was to change the world:

> For me, the play is not the thing … 'For art's sake' alone I would not face the toil of writing a single sentence.'

> Preface to **Man and Superman**, 1903

Introduction

The Devil's Disciple comes from the first period of Shaw's playwriting career, and although it is a rewarding and entertaining play, it is not one of his most celebrated works. It has rather fallen out of favour with theatrical producers in recent years, although it is perhaps significant that the Royal National Theatre in London revived it in 1994. It was first produced in America, in 1897, with a first London production in 1899. The American production was very successful, and brought Shaw over £2000, a considerable sum in those days.

The play was published in 1901 as one of three plays in a collection entitled *Three Plays for Puritans*. The other two plays are *Captain Brassbound's Conversion*, another melodrama, and *Caesar and Cleopatra*, a version of the relationship between the two historical characters. Shaw had already published a collection, *Plays Pleasant and Unpleasant*, following his decision to gain a wider audience for his work by presenting the plays so that they might be read like novels.

Puritanism

In the Preface to the play, Shaw explains why he has called this collection *Plays for Puritans*. He is vehemently opposed, as were the Puritans, to the 'drama of romance and sensuality'. But Shaw wanted to replace it with a theatre of ideas, one in which characters could present opposing views and in which there was not necessarily any clear resolution of the real problems of the world. He disliked what he felt to be the life-denying aspect of Puritanism: the compulsion to follow one, strict, laid-down law. The life-affirming character of Dick Dudgeon is one of the central themes of *The Devil's Disciple*, and we are given, in Act 3, the chance to consider whether he has been a hero or a fool, by comparing his actions with those of the clergyman, Anthony Anderson.

Mrs Dudgeon, Dick's mother, is a grim representation of 'the barren forms and observances of a dead Puritanism' (Act 1, page 23). This was the rigidly severe Puritanism that disapproved of the theatre, as well as many other forms of entertainment, in principle. Theatres were in fact closed during the period of the Commonwealth in seventeen-century Britain, after the defeat of King Charles I by the largely Puritan Parliamentary forces.

Shaw's own religious views were unconventional. He did not believe in an all-powerful God, but in a 'Life Force' and the need for people to search within themselves for principles by which to live. According to Shaw's theory of 'creative evolution', which he expounded in several later plays and articles, progress and the very survival of humanity depend on the power of rational ideas and of the will to assist the Life Force.

Shaw was, however, very familiar with the King James Bible, and regarded it as a great work of literature. *The Devil's Disciple* is full of quotations from, and references to, the Bible, as one might expect in the speech of the Puritan colonists. Shaw does not explicitly condemn religion in the play, but he shows that what matters is how people actually behave rather than what their professed religious beliefs are.

Melodrama

It is rare today to see a melodrama performed except perhaps by amateur companies for historical interest or for amusement. *East Lynne* by Mrs Henry Wood is one of those often revived; it contains the immortal line 'Dead, dead, and never called me Mother!'). In the nineteenth century melodramas were a very popular form of entertainment for the middle and lower classes, and certain theatres and actors specialised in this form of drama. The name comes from the fact that originally the play was performed with incidental music, and each leading character had a 'signature tune' which reinforced the impression he or she was trying to make of being brave or villainous and so on. The plots could perhaps be summarised as: good, after much adversity, triumphs over evil. The heroes and heroines were often poor, and the villains often rich or upper-class. For example, the villainous landlord throws the poor family out of their house into the snow, but is eventually brought down by the poor man exposing a shameful secret from the landlord's past. The melodramas made a crude appeal to the emotions, and because they usually had a happy ending were a form of escapism for audiences whose own lives were far from comfortable or secure. Shaw was approached in 1896 by William Terriss to write a melodrama for him to perform with his company at the Adelphi Theatre. Terriss had been a member of Sir Henry Irving's company, but now was very successful at the Adelphi, which had become the home of melodrama. Terriss usually played the hero, and his mistress, Jessie Millward, the heroine. Terriss suggested a fanciful plot which involved the hanging of the hero at the end, a hanging which turns out simply to have been a nightmare. Shaw was very reluctant to take up Terriss's suggestion, but did not want to offend him, and proposed writing something different. Shaw however later returned to the idea of a melodrama, and worked on it during 1896. He was aware of the danger that his ideas would become submerged beneath the audience's easy acceptance of the melodramatic conventions. He wrote:

> *Every old patron of the Adelphi pit would... recognize the reading of the Will, the oppressed orphan finding a protector, the arrest, the heroic sacrifice, the court martial, the scaffold, the reprieve at the last moment, as he recognizes beefsteak pudding on the bill of fare at his restaurant.*

When Shaw took the play to Terriss, the actor could not recall his suggestion of a melodrama, and even fell asleep while Shaw was reading the play to him. Shaw still wanted Terriss to produce it, but then unfortunately Terriss was murdered by a lunatic on the steps of the Adelphi – he died in Jessie Millward's arms. So the play was first performed in America by the actor-manager Richard Mansfield, who had enjoyed a previous success with **Arms and the Man**. Shaw claimed to have written the play 'with one eye on Terriss and the other on Richard Mansfield', although he warned Mansfield that the play would probably fail, particularly the third Act. (Shaw once wrote to the famous English actress Ellen Terry: 'I think I shall die lonely as far as my third acts are concerned').

Rebellion

In Shaw's original sketches for the play, no specific country or period is mentioned, and it is not clear when he decided to set it in the New England of 1777. He may indeed have had an eye on Mansfield in America, but whatever the reason, setting it against the rebellion of the American colonies is evidence of Shaw's care in fashioning his plays. He is able to set Dick, a human rebel against his family and its religion also against conventional morality on the wider stage of the events surrounding the colonists who opposed their rulers.

The play should not be seen as an accurate historical record. Shaw took most of his facts from De Fonblanque's biography of Burgoyne, but even then he took several liberties with his character and actions. For example, in Act 3, Shaw gives Burgoyne pre-knowledge of his eventual surrender at Saratoga. Burgoyne remarks that in Anderson the rebels may have found a leader, thus ignoring the actual leaders, George Washington and Benedict Arnold. Shaw appears to have made up the nickname of 'Gentlemanly Johnny' for Burgoyne, and historians have subsequently copied it, in a nice illustration of Burgoyne's remark (Act 3, page 88), that 'History ... will tell lies, as usual'.

Dick Dudgeon is undoubtedly regarded as a rebel, and in Act 1 he reinforces this reputation by the way he speaks to and treats his relatives. He takes Essie, the illegitimate daughter of his uncle, under his protection. But apart from Mrs Dudgeon's description in Act 1 of his association with gypsies, smugglers and villains, nothing specific is ever alleged against him. Of course, for the true believers of the

Puritan community, Dick's rejection of their religion and his proclamation of himself as the Devil's Disciple would have been enough to condemn him as an unrepentant and dangerous sinner – dangerous because he challenges all their notions of what is right, what is proper, and above all he threatens their security. Dick's philosophy can perhaps be seen as part of the natural rebellion of the young against their parents, but Dick is rather older than the usual 'teenage rebel'.

The hero and the villain

Every melodrama needs a hero. So do many other plays and novels, and there is no doubt that in the first two Acts of **The Devil's Disciple** Dick Dudgeon is the hero, in the sense that all the action revolves around him, that he dominates the other characters. In Act 1, from the moment that he enters for the reading of the will, he controls the situation, asserts his dominance over his family and, in the words of Lawyer Hawkins is 'cock of the walk'. By Act 3, when he is on trial for his life, his demeanour has changed, to one of quiet resolution, professing indifference to his fate on the gallows. He still asserts his moral superiority, particularly in his verbal duels with General Burgoyne, but by the end of the play it is less clear whether Dick is indeed a hero, someone to be looked up to, or a fool who has allowed himself to be deceived by a romantic notion of self-sacrifice. Anthony Anderson is seen as the man of action, the leader who has thrown off the passivity of his clergyman's role, and Dick says bitterly of himself that he has behaved like a fool. The transition in Anderson is rather too quick to be truly believable, but it is clear that Dick's role is not simply that of the traditional melodramatic hero.

The self-sacrifice of Dick is at the heart of the play, and it has been often discussed and analysed by theatre critics. The most obvious parallel is that of Christ, giving his life to save mankind, and the notion of a self-proclaimed disciple of the devil, God's enemy, behaving in the same way, is one that would obviously have appealed to Shaw, both because of its perversity and because of Shaw's opposition to organised established religion. The major unresolved question is whether Dick's action is believable either in real life or in the context of the play.

Charles Dickens's novel **A Tale of Two Cities** contains a well-known similar example of self-sacrifice. Sidney Carton, a dissolute English lawyer, is guillotined in place of Charles Darnay, a French aristocrat. He allows himself to be killed partly as a way of giving some meaning to a wasted life, but mainly because of his undeclared love for Darnay's wife. Carton's speech from the scaffold has entered the English language: 'It is a far, far better thing I do than I have ever done'. Dickens's novel had been turned into several play versions, and Shaw would have been very familiar with the story. Michael Holroyd points out that unlike conventional heroes, including Carton, who would have sacrificed themselves for love, Dick denies acting out of love. He says, 'That has taught me to set very little store by the goodness that only comes out red hot. What I did last night, I did in cold blood' (Act 3, page 72). Shaw said in a letter over ten years after writing the play:

> The only aim that is at all peculiar to me is my disregard of warm feelings. They are quite well able to take care of themselves. What I want is a race of men who can be kind in cold blood. Anybody can be kind in emotional moments.

Letter to Mrs O'Byrne, 14 October 1909

The role of villain in the play is less clear-cut. Mrs Dudgeon is portrayed as an unpleasant and embittered woman, but she could hardly be said to be villainous. Besides, Shaw removes her from the play pretty smartly, having her die off-stage once she has played her part in establishing the background against which Dick is rebelling. The British are undoubtedly shown as cruel and incompetent, and their leader General Burgoyne is cynical. But he appears only in Act 3, rather late to introduce a villain, and at the end of the play he seems to have accepted his defeat with equanimity, inviting Dick and Judith Anderson to lunch.

The role of women

The women in **The Devil's Disciple** are restricted to the domestic setting. They had little legal or political status, and, if married, were regarded as scarcely better than the possessions of their husbands. However, the women are not mere ciphers; they see through the crude notions of the men, though there is little they can do to alter the circumstances. Shaw was a strong supporter of the rights of women, as shown by his remarks at the conclusion of the reading of the will (Act 1, page 43).

Stage directions and punctuation

Shaw took great pains over the printing of his plays and insisted that stage directions should always be in italics. This meant that when he wanted a character to emphasise a word, it had to be written in a different way. Shaw chose to space out the letters, for example in Act 1, page 36:

UNCLE TITUS   Well, I hope he will have the grace not to come, I h o p e so.

Shaw was also particular about spelling. He insisted that apostrophes should not be used, so that 'I shan't' becomes 'I shant'; 'don't' becomes 'dont', and so on. (However, Shaw still uses I'm and it's.) Throughout his life, Shaw campaigned for a more logical spelling of English words and so he uses color, honor, etc.

Reading log

One of the easiest ways of keeping track of your reading is to keep a log book. This can be any exercise book or folder that you have to hand, but make sure you reserve it exclusively for reflecting on your reading, both at home and in school.

As you read the play, stop from time to time and think back over what you have read.

- Is there anything that puzzles you? Note down some questions that you might want to research, discuss with your friends or ask a teacher. Also note any quotations which strike you as important or memorable.

- Does your reading remind you of anything else you have read, heard or seen on TV or the cinema? Jot down what it is and where the similarities lie.

- Have you had any experiences similar to those narrated in the play? Do you find yourself identifying closely with one or more of the characters? Record this as accurately as you can.

- Do you find yourself really liking, or really loathing, any of the characters? What is it about them that makes you feel so strongly? Make notes that you can add to.

- Can you picture the locations and settings? Draw maps, plans, diagrams, drawings, in fact any doodle that helps you make sense of these things.

- Now and again try to predict what will happen next in the plot. Use what you already know of the author, the genre (type of story) and the characters to help you do this. Later record how close you were and whether you were surprised at the outcome.

- Write down any feelings that you have about the play. Your reading log should help you to make sense of your own ideas alongside those of the author.

The Devil's Disciple

CHARACTERS

in the order of their appearance

MRS DUDGEON
THE GIRL/ESSIE
CHRISTY
ANTHONY ANDERSON
JUDITH ANDERSON
LAWYER HAWKINS
UNCLE WILLIAM DUDGEON
UNCLE TITUS DUDGEON
RICHARD DUDGEON
MRS WILLIAM DUDGEON
MRS TITUS DUDGEON
THE SERGEANT
MAJOR SWINDON
GENERAL BURGOYNE
CHAPLAIN/MR BRUDENELL
SOLDIERS

SHAW'S PREFACE

Why for Puritans? [1]

Since I gave my Plays, Pleasant and Unpleasant, to the world two years ago, many things have happened to me. I had then just entered on the fourth year of my activity as a critic of the London theatres. They very nearly killed me. I had survived seven years of London's music, four or five years of London's pictures, and about as much of its current literature, wrestling critically with them with all my force and skill. After that, the criticism of the theatre came to me as a huge relief in point of bodily exertion. The difference between the leisure of a Persian cat and the labor of a cockney cab horse is not greater than the difference between the official weekly or fortnightly playgoings of the theatre critic and the restless daily rushing to and fro of the music critic, from the stroke of three in the afternoon, when the concerts begin, to the stroke of twelve at night, when the opera ends. The pictures were nearly as bad. An Alpinist once, noticing the massive soles of my boots, asked me whether I climbed mountains. No, I replied: these boots are for the hard floors of the London galleries. Yet I once dealt with music and pictures together in the spare time of an active young revolutionist, and wrote plays and books and other toilsome things into the bargain. But the theatre struck me down like the veriest weakling. I sank under it like a baby fed on starch. My very bones began to perish, so that I had to get them planed and gouged by accomplished surgeons. I fell from heights and broke my limbs in pieces. The doctors said: This man has not eaten meat for twenty years: he must eat it or die. I said: This man has been going to the London theatres for

[1] *The Devil's Disciple*, written in 1897, was published in *Three Plays for Puritans* in 1900, together with *Caesar and Cleopatra* and *Captain Brassbound's Conversion*. The present edition omits the last section of Shaw's Preface, headed 'Better than Shakespear?' and relating only to *Caesar and Cleopatra*.

three years; and the soul of him has become inane and is feeding unnaturally on his body. And I was right. I did not change my diet; but I had myself carried up into a mountain where there was no theatre; and there I began to revive. Too weak to work, I wrote books and plays: hence the second and third plays in this volume. And now I am stronger than I have been at any moment since my feet first carried me as a critic across the fatal threshold of a London playhouse.

Why was this? What is the matter with the theatre, that a strong man can die of it? Well, the answer will make a long story; but it must be told. And, to begin, why have I just called the theatre a playhouse? The well-fed Englishman, though he lives and dies a schoolboy, cannot play. He cannot even play cricket or football: he has to work at them: that is why he beats the foreigner who plays at them. To him playing means playing the fool. He can hunt and shoot and travel and fight: he can, when special holiday festivity is suggested to him, eat and drink, dice and drab, smoke and lounge. But play he cannot. The moment you make his theatre a place of amusement instead of a place of edification, you make it, not a real playhouse, but a place of excitement for the sportsman and the sensualist.

However, this well-fed grown-up-schoolboy Englishman counts for little in the modern metropolitan audience. In the long lines of waiting playgoers lining the pavements outside our fashionable theatres every evening, the men are only the currants in the dumpling. Women are in the majority; and women and men alike belong to that least robust of all our social classes, the class which earns from eighteen to thirty shillings a week in sedentary employment, and lives in lonely lodgings or in drab homes with nagging relatives. These people preserve the innocence of the theatre: they have neither the philosopher's impatience to get to realities (reality being the one thing they want to escape from), nor the longing of the sportsman for violent action, nor the full-fed, experienced, disillusioned sensuality of the rich man, whether he be gentleman or sporting publican.

WHY FOR PURITANS?

They read a good deal, and are at home in the fool's paradise of popular romance. They love the pretty man and the pretty woman, and will have both of them fashionably dressed and exquisitely idle, posing against backgrounds of drawing room and dainty garden; in love, but sentimentally, romantically; always ladylike and gentlemanlike. Jejunely insipid, all this, to the stalls, which are paid for (when they *are* paid for) by people who have their own dresses and drawing rooms, and know them to be a mere masquerade behind which there is nothing romantic, and little that is interesting to most of the masqueraders except the clandestine play of natural licentiousness.

The stalls cannot be fully understood without taking into account the absence of the rich evangelical English merchant and his family, and the presence of the rich Jewish merchant and *his* family. I can see no validity whatever in the view that the influence of the rich Jews on the theatre is any worse than the influence of the rich of any other race. Other qualities being equal, men become rich in commerce in proportion to the intensity and exclusiveness of their desire for money. It may be a misfortune that the purchasing power of men who value money above art, philosophy, and the welfare of the whole community, should enable them to influence the theatre (and everything else in the market); but there is no reason to suppose that their influence is any nobler when they imagine themselves Christians than when they know themselves Jews. All that can fairly be said of the Jewish influence on the theatre is that it is exotic, and is not only a customer's influence but a financier's influence: so much so, that the way is smoothest for those plays and those performers that appeal specially to the Jewish taste. English influence on the theatre, as far as the stalls are concerned, does not exist, because the rich purchasing-powerful Englishman prefers politics and church-going: his soul is too stubborn to be purged by an avowed make-believe. When he wants sensuality he practises it: he does not play with voluptuous or romantic ideas. From the play of ideas—and the drama can never be anything more—he demands edification, and will not pay for anything else in that arena. Consequently the box office will never become an English influence until the theatre turns from the drama of romance and sensuality to the drama of edification.

Turning from the stalls to the whole auditorium, consider what is implied by the fact that the prices (all much too high, by the way) range from half a guinea to a shilling, the ages from eighteen to eighty, whilst every age, and nearly every price, represents a different taste. Is it not clear that this diversity in the audience makes it impossible to gratify every one of its units by the same luxury, since in that domain of infinite caprice, one man's meat is another man's poison, one age's longing another age's loathing? And yet that is just what the theatres kept trying to do almost all the time I was doomed to attend them. On the other hand, to interest people of divers ages, classes, and temperaments by some generally momentous subject of thought, as the politicians and preachers do, would seem the most obvious course in the world. And yet the theatres avoided that as a ruinous eccentricity. Their wiseacres persisted in assuming that all men have the same tastes, fancies, and qualities of passion; that no two have the same interests; and that most playgoers have no interests at all. This being precisely contrary to the obvious facts, it followed that the majority of the plays produced were failures, recognizable as such before the end of the first act by the very wiseacres aforementioned, who, quite incapable of understanding the lesson, would thereupon set to work to obtain and produce a play applying their theory still more strictly, with proportionately more disastrous results. The sums of money I saw thus transferred from the pockets of theatrical speculators and syndicates to those of wigmakers, costumiers, scene painters, carpenters, doorkeepers, actors, theatre landlords, and all the other people for whose exclusive benefit most London theatres seem to exist, would have kept a theatre devoted exclusively to the highest drama open all the year round. If the Browning and Shelley Societies were fools, as the wiseacres said they were, for producing Strafford, Colombe's Birthday, and The Cenci; if the Independent Theatre, the New Century Theatre, and the Stage Society are impracticable faddists for producing the plays of Ibsen and Maeterlinck, then what epithet is contemptuous enough for the people who produce the would-be popular plays?

The actor-managers were far more successful, because they produced plays that at least pleased themselves, whereas Commerce, with a false theory of how to please everybody, produced plays that pleased nobody. But their occasional personal successes in voluptuous plays, and, in any case, their careful concealment of failure, confirmed the prevalent error, which was exposed fully only when the plays had to stand or fall openly by their own merits. Even Shakespear was played with his brains cut out. In 1896, when Sir Henry Irving was disabled by an accident at a moment when Miss Ellen Terry was too ill to appear, the theatre had to be closed after a brief attempt to rely on the attraction of a Shakespearean play performed by the stock company. This may have been Shakespear's fault: indeed Sir Henry later on complained that he had lost a princely sum by Shakespear. But Shakespear's reply to this, if he were able to make it, would be that the princely sum was spent, not on his dramatic poetry, but on a gorgeous stage ritualism superimposed on reckless mutilations of his text, the whole being addressed to a public as to which nothing is certain except that its natural bias is towards reverence for Shakespear and dislike and distrust of ritualism. No doubt the Irving ritual appealed to a far more cultivated sensuousness and imaginativeness than the musical farces in which our stage Abbots of Misrule pontificated (with the same financially disastrous result); but in both there was the same intentional brainlessness, founded on the same theory that the public did not want brains, did not want to think, did not want anything but pleasure at the theatre. Unfortunately, this theory happens to be true of a certain section of the public. This section, being courted by the theatres, went to them and drove the other people out. It then discovered, as any expert could have foreseen, that the theatre cannot compete in mere pleasuremongering either with the other arts or with matter-of-fact gallantry. Stage pictures are the worst pictures, stage music the worst music, stage scenery the worst scenery within reach of the Londoner. The leading lady or gentleman may be as tempting to the admirer in the pit as the dishes in a cookshop window are to the penniless tramp on the pavement; but people do not, I presume, go to the theatre to be merely tantalized.

The breakdown on the last point was conclusive. For when the managers tried to put their principle of pleasing everybody into practice, Necessity, ever ironical towards Folly, had driven them to seek a universal pleasure to appeal to. And since many have no ear for music or eye for color, the search for universality inevitably flung the managers back on the instinct of sex as the avenue to all hearts. Of course the appeal was a vapid failure. Speaking for my own sex, I can say that the leading lady was not to everybody's taste: her pretty face often became ugly when she tried to make it expressive; her voice lost its charm (if it ever had any) when she had nothing sincere to say; and the stalls, from racial prejudice, were apt to insist on more Rebecca and less Rowena than the pit cared for. It may seem strange, even monstrous, that a man should feel a constant attachment to the hideous witches in Macbeth, and yet yawn at the prospect of spending another evening in the contemplation of a beauteous young leading lady with voluptuous contours and longlashed eyes, painted and dressed to perfection in the latest fashions. But that is just what happened to me in the theatre.

I did not find that matters were improved by the lady pretending to be "a woman with a past," violently oversexed, or the play being called a problem play, even when the manager, and sometimes, I suspect, the very author, firmly believed the word problem to be the latest euphemism for what Justice Shallow called a bona roba, and certainly would not either of them have staked a farthing on the interest of a genuine problem. In fact these so-called problem plays invariably depended for their dramatic interest on foregone conclusions of the most heartwearying conventionality concerning sexual morality. The authors had no problematic views: all they wanted was to capture some of the fascination of Ibsen. It seemed to them that most of Ibsen's heroines were naughty ladies. And they tried to produce Ibsen plays by making their heroines naughty. But they took great care to make them pretty and expensively dressed. Thus the pseudo-Ibsen play was nothing but the ordinary sensuous ritual of the stage become as frankly pornographic as good manners allowed.

I found that the whole business of stage sensuousness, whether as Lyceum Shakespear, musical farce, or sham Ibsen, finally disgusted me, not because I was Pharisaical, or intolerantly refined, but because I was bored; and boredom is a condition which makes men as susceptible to disgust and irritation as headache makes them to noise and glare. Being a man, I have my share of the masculine silliness and vulgarity on the subject of sex which so astonishes women, to whom sex is a serious matter. I am not an archbishop, and do not pretend to pass my life on one plane or in one mood, and that the highest: on the contrary, I am, I protest, as accessible to the humors of The Rogue's Comedy or The Rake's Progress as to the pious decencies of The Sign of the Cross. Thus Falstaff, coarser than any of the men in our loosest plays, does not bore me: Doll Tearsheet, more abandoned than any of the women, does not shock me. I admit that Romeo and Juliet would be a duller play if it were robbed of the solitary fragment it has preserved for us of the conversation of the husband of Juliet's nurse. No: my disgust was not mere thinskinned prudery. When my moral sense revolted, as it often did to the very fibres, it was invariably at the nauseous compliances of the theatre with conventional virtue. If I despised the musical farces, it was because they never had the courage of their vices. With all their labored efforts to keep up an understanding of furtive naughtiness between the low comedian on the stage and the drunken undergraduate in the stalls, they insisted all the time on their virtue and patriotism and loyalty as pitifully as a poor girl of the pavement will pretend to be a clergyman's daughter. True, I may have been offended when a manager, catering for me with coarse frankness as a slave dealer caters for a Pasha, invited me to forget the common bond of humanity between me and his company by demanding nothing from them but a gloatably voluptuous appearance. But this extreme is never reached at our better theatres. The shop assistants, the typists, the clerks, who, as I have said, preserve the innocence of the theatre, would not dare to let themselves be pleased by it. Even if they did, they would not get it from our reputable managers, who, when faced with the only logical conclusion from their principle of making the theatre a temple of pleasure, indignantly refuse to change the theatrical profession for Mrs Warren's. For that is what all this demand for pleasure at the theatre finally comes to; and the answer to it is, not that people ought not to desire sensuous pleasure (they cannot help it) but that the theatre cannot give it to them, even to the extent permitted by the honor and conscience of the best managers, because a theatre is so far from being a pleasant or even a comfortable place that only by making us forget ourselves can it prevent us from realizing its inconveniences. A play that does not do this for the pleasure-seeker allows him to discover that he has chosen a disagreeable and expensive way of spending the evening. He wants to drink, to smoke, to change the spectacle, to get rid of the middle-aged actor and actress who are boring him, and to see shapely young dancing girls and acrobats doing more amusing things in a more plastic manner. In short, he wants the music hall; and he goes there, leaving the managers astonished at this unexpected but quite inevitable result of the attempt to please him. Whereas, had he been enthralled by the play, even with horror, instead of himself enthralling with the dread of his displeasure the manager, the author and the actors, all had been well. And so we must conclude that the theatre is a place which people can endure only when they forget themselves: that is, when their attention is entirely captured, their interest thoroughly aroused, their sympathies raised to the eagerest readiness, and their selfishness utterly annihilated. Imagine, then, the result of conducting theatres on the principle of appealing exclusively to the instinct of self-gratification in people without power of attention, without interests, without sympathy: in short, without brains or heart. That is how they were conducted whilst I was writing about them; and that is how they nearly killed me.

Yet the managers mean well. Their self-respect is in excess rather than in defect; for they are in full reaction against the Bohemianism of past generations of actors, and so bent on compelling social recognition by a blameless respectability, that the drama, neglected in the struggle, is only just beginning to stir feebly after standing still in England from Tom Robertson's time in the sixties until the first actor was knighted in the nineties. The manager may not want good plays; but he does not want bad plays: he wants nice ones. Nice plays, with nice dresses, nice drawing rooms and nice people, are indispensable: to be ungenteel is worse than to fail. I use the word ungenteel purposely; for the stage presents life on thirty pounds a day, not as it is, but as it is conceived by the earners of thirty shillings a week. The real thing would shock the audience exactly as the manners of the public school and university shock a Board of Guardians. In just the same way, the plays which constitute the genuine aristocracy of modern dramatic literature shock the reverence for gentility which governs our theatres today. For instance, the objection to Ibsen is not really an objection to his philosophy: it is a protest against the fact that his characters do not behave as ladies and gentlemen are popularly supposed to behave. If you adore Hedda Gabler in real life, if you envy her and feel that nothing but your poverty prevents you from being as exquisite a creature, if you know that the accident of matrimony (say with an officer of the guards who falls in love with you across the counter whilst you are reckoning the words in his telegram) may at any moment put you in her place, Ibsen's exposure of the worthlessness and meanness of her life is cruel and blasphemous to you. This point of view is not caught by the clever ladies of Hedda's own class, who recognize the portrait, applaud its painter, and think the fuss against Ibsen means nothing more than the conventional disapproval of her discussions of a *ménage a trois* with Judge Brack. A little experience of popular plays would soon convince these clever ladies that a heroine who atones in the last act by committing suicide may do all the things that Hedda only talked about, without a word of remonstrance from the press or the public. It is not murder, not adultery, not rapine that is objected to: quite the contrary. It is an unladylike attitude towards life: in other words, a disparagement of the social ideals of the poorer middle class and of the vast reinforcements it has had from the working class during the last twenty years. Let but the attitude of the author be gentlemanlike, and his heroines may do what they please. Mrs Tanqueray was received with delight by the public: Saint Teresa would have been hissed off the same stage for her contempt for the ideal represented by a carriage, a fashionable dressmaker, and a dozen servants.

Here, then, is a pretty problem for the manager. He is convinced that plays must depend for their dramatic force on appeals to the sex instinct; and yet he owes it to his own newly conquered social position that they shall be perfectly genteel plays, fit for churchgoers. The sex instinct must therefore proceed upon genteel assumptions. Impossible! you will exclaim. But you are wrong: nothing is more astonishing than the extent to which, in real life, the sex instinct does so proceed, even when the consequence is its lifelong starvation. Few of us have vitality enough to make any of our instincts imperious: we can be made to live on pretences, as the masterful minority well know. But the timid majority, if it rules nowhere else, at least rules in the theatre: fitly enough too, because on the stage pretence is all that can exist. Life has its realities behind its shows: the theatre has nothing but its shows. But can the theatre make a show of lovers' endearments? A thousand times no: perish the thought of such unladylike, ungentlemanlike exhibitions. You can have fights, rescues, conflagrations, trials-at-law, avalanches, murders and executions all directly simulated on the stage if you will. But any such realistic treatment of the incidents of sex is quite out of the question. The singer, the dramatic dancer, the exquisite declaimer of impassioned poesy, the rare artist who, bringing something of the art of all three to the ordinary work of the theatre, can enthral an audience by the expression of dramatic feeling alone, may take love for a theme on the stage; but the prosaic walking gentleman of our fashionable theatres, realistically simulating the incidents of life, cannot touch it without indecorum.

Can any dilemma be more complete? Love is assumed to be the only theme that touches all your audience infallibly, young and old, rich and poor. And yet love is the one subject that the drawing room drama dare not present.

Out of this dilemma, which is a very old one, has come the romantic play: that is, the play in which love is carefully kept off the stage, whilst it is alleged as the motive of all the actions presented to the audience. The result is, to me at least, an intolerable perversion of human conduct. There are two classes of stories that seem to me to be not only fundamentally false but sordidly base. One is the pseudo-religious story, in which the hero or heroine does good on strictly commercial grounds, reluctantly exercising a little virtue on earth in consideration of receiving in return an exorbitant payment in heaven: much as if an odalisque were to allow a cadi to whip her for a couple of millions in gold. The other is the romance in which the hero, also rigidly commercial, will do nothing except for the sake of the heroine. Surely this is as depressing as it is unreal. Compare with it the treatment of love, frankly indecent according to our notions, in oriental fiction. In the Arabian Nights we have a series of stories, some of them very good ones, in which no sort of decorum is observed. The result is that they are infinitely more instructive and enjoyable than our romances, because love is treated in them as naturally as any other passion. There is no cast iron convention as to its effects; no false association of general depravity of character with its corporealities or of general eleva-tion with its sentimentalities; no pretence that a man or woman cannot be courageous and kind and friendly unless infatuatedly in love with somebody (is no poet manly enough to sing The Old Maids of England?): rather, indeed, an insistence on the blinding and narrowing power of lovesickness to make princely heroes unhappy and unfortunate. These tales expose, further, the delusion that the interest of this most capricious, most transient, most easily baffled of all instincts, is inexhaustible, and that the field of the English romancer has been cruelly narrowed by the restrictions under which he is permitted to deal with it. The Arabian storyteller, relieved of all such restrictions, heaps char-acter on character, adventure on adventure, marvel on marvel; whilst the English novelist, like the starving tramp who can think of nothing but his hunger, seems to be unable to escape from the obsession of sex, and will rewrite the very gospels because the originals are not written in the sensuously ecstatic style. At the instance of Martin Luther we long ago gave up imposing celibacy on our priests; but we still impose it on our art, with the very undesirable and unexpected result that no editor, publisher, or manager, will now accept a story or produce a play without "love interest" in it. Take, for a recent example, Mr H. G. Wells's War of the Worlds, a tale of the invasion of the earth by the inhabitants of the planet Mars: a capital story, not to be laid down until finished. Love interest is impossible on its scientific plane: nothing could be more impertinent and irritating. Yet Mr Wells has had to pretend that the hero is in love with a young lady manufactured for the purpose, and to imply that it is on her account alone that he feels concerned about the apparently in-evitable destruction of the human race by the Martians. Another example. An American novelist, recently deceased, made a hit some years ago by compiling a Bostonian Utopia from the pros-pectuses of the little bands of devout Communists who have from time to time, since the days of Fourier and Owen, tried to establish millennial colonies outside our commercial civilization. Even in this economic Utopia we find the inevitable love affair. The hero, waking up in a distant future from a miraculous sleep, meets a Boston young lady, provided expressly for him to fall in love with. Women have by that time given up wearing skirts; but she, to spare his delicacy, gets one out of a museum of antiquities to wear in his presence until he is hardened to the customs of the new age. When I came to that touching incident, I became as Paolo and Francesca: "in that book I read no more." I will not multiply examples: if such unendurable follies occur in the sort of story made by working out a meteorological or economic hypothesis, the extent to which it is carried in sentimental romances needs no expatiation.

The worst of it is that since man's intellectual consciousness of himself is derived from the descriptions of him in books, a persistent misrepresentation of humanity in literature gets finally accepted and acted upon. If every mirror reflected our noses twice their natural size, we should live and die in the faith that we were all Punches; and we should scout a true mirror as the work of a fool, madman, or jester. Nay, I believe we should, by Lamarckian adaptation, enlarge our noses to the admired size; for I have noticed that when a certain type of feature appears in painting and is admired as beautiful, it presently becomes common in nature; so that the Beatrices and Francescas in the picture galleries of one generation, to whom minor poets address verses entitled To My Lady, come to life as the parlormaids and waitresses of the next. If the conventions of romance are only insisted on long enough and uniformly enough (a condition guaranteed by the uniformity of human folly and vanity), then, for the huge compulsorily schooled masses who read romance or nothing, these conventions will become the laws of personal honor. Jealousy, which is either an egotistical meanness or a specific mania, will become obligatory; and ruin, ostracism, breaking up of homes, duelling, murder, suicide and infanticide will be produced (often have been produced, in fact) by incidents which, if left to the operation of natural and right feeling, would produce nothing worse than an hour's soon-forgotten fuss. Men will be slain needlessly on the field of battle because officers conceive it to be their first duty to make romantic exhibitions of conspicuous gallantry. The squire who has never spared an hour from the hunting field to do a little public work on a parish council will be cheered as a patriot because he is willing to kill and get killed for the sake of conferring himself as an institution on other countries. In the courts cases will be argued, not on juridical but on romantic principles; and vindictive damages and vindictive sentences, with the acceptance of nonsensical, and the repudiation or suppression of sensible testimony, will destroy the very sense of law. Kaisers, generals, judges, and prime ministers will set the example of playing to the gallery. Finally the people, now that their compulsory literacy enables every penman to play on their romantic illusions, will be led by the nose far more completely than they ever were by playing on their former ignorance and superstition. Nay, why should I say will be? they *are*. Ten years of cheap reading have changed the English from the most stolid nation in Europe to the most theatrical and hysterical.

It is clear now, why the theatre was insufferable to me; why it left its black mark on my bones as it has left its black mark on the character of the nation; why I call the Puritans to rescue it again as they rescued it before when its foolish pursuit of pleasure sunk it in "profaneness and immorality"? I have, I think, always been a Puritan in my attitude towards Art. I am as fond of fine music and handsome building as Milton was, or Cromwell, or Bunyan; but if I found that they were becoming the instruments of a systematic idolatry of sensuousness, I would hold it good statesmanship to blow every cathedral in the world to pieces with dynamite, organ and all, without the least heed to the screams of the art critics and cultured voluptuaries. And when I see that the nineteenth century has crowned the idolatry of Art with the deification of Love, so that every poet is supposed to have pierced to the holy of holies when he has announced that Love is the Supreme, or the Enough, or the All, I feel that Art was safer in the hands of the most fanatical of Cromwell's major generals than it will be if ever it gets into mine. The pleasures of the senses I can sympathize with and share; but the substitution of sensuous ecstasy for intellectual activity and honesty is the very devil. It has already brought us to Flogging Bills in Parliament, and, by reaction, to androgynous heroes on the stage; and if the infection spreads until the democratic attitude becomes thoroughly Romanticist, the country will become unbearable for all realists, Philistine or Platonic. When it comes to that, the brute force of the strong-minded Bismarckian man of action, impatient of humbug, will combine with the subtlety and spiritual energy of the man of thought whom shams cannot illude or interest. That combination will be on one side; and Romanticism will be on the other. In which event, so much the worse for Romanticism, which will come down even if it has to drag Democracy down with it. For all institutions have in the long run to live by the nature of things, and not by childish pretendings.

ON DIABOLONIAN ETHICS

There is a foolish opinion prevalent that an author should allow his works to speak for themselves, and that he who appends and prefixes explanations to them is likely to be as bad an artist as the painter cited by Cervantes, who wrote under his picture This is a Cock, lest there should be any mistake about it. The pat retort to this thoughtless comparison is that the painter invariably does so label his picture. What is a Royal Academy catalogue but a series of statements that This is The Vale of Rest, This The Shaving of Samson, This Chill October, This H.R.H. The Prince of Wales, and so on? The reason most playwrights do not publish their plays with prefaces is that they cannot write them, the business of intellectually conscious philosopher and skilled critic being no necessary part of their craft. Naturally,

15

making a virtue of their incapacity, they either repudiate prefaces as shameful, or else, with a modest air, request some popular critic to supply one, as much as to say, Were I to tell the truth about myself I must needs seem vainglorious: were I to tell less than the truth I should do myself an injustice and deceive my readers. As to the critic thus called in from the outside, what can he do but imply that his friend's transcendent ability as a dramatist is surpassed only by his beautiful nature as a man? Now what I say is, why should I get another man to praise me when I can praise myself? I have no disabilities to plead: produce me your best critic, and I will criticize his head off. As to philosophy, I taught my critics the little they know in my Quintessence of Ibsenism; and now they turn their guns—the guns I loaded for them—on me, and proclaim that I write as if mankind had intellect without will, or heart, as they call it. Ingrates: who was it that directed your attention to the distinction between Will and Intellect? Not Schopenhauer, I think, but Shaw.

Again, they tell me that So-and-So, who does not write prefaces, is no charlatan. Well, I am. I first caught the ear of the British public on a cart in Hyde Park, to the blaring of brass bands, and this not at all as a reluctant sacrifice of my instinct of privacy to political necessity, but because, like all dramatists and mimes of genuine vocation, I am a natural-born mountebank. I am well aware that the ordinary British citizen requires a profession of shame from all mountebanks by way of homage to the sanctity of the ignoble private life to which he is condemned by his incapacity for public life. Thus Shakespear, after proclaiming that Not marble nor the gilded monuments of Princes should outlive his powerful rhyme, would apologize, in the approved taste, for making himself a motley to the view; and the British citizen has ever since quoted the apology and ignored the fanfare. When an actress writes her memoirs, she impresses on you in every chapter how cruelly it tried her feelings to exhibit her person to the public gaze; but she does not forget to decorate the book with a dozen portraits of herself. I really cannot respond to this demand for mock-modesty. I am ashamed neither of my work nor of the way it is done. I like explaining its merits to the huge majority who dont know good work from bad. It does them good; and it does me good, curing me of nervousness, laziness, and snobbishness. I write prefaces as Dryden did, and treatises as Wagner, because I *can*; and I would give half a dozen of Shakespear's plays for one of the prefaces he ought to have written. I leave the delicacies of retirement to those who are gentlemen first and literary workmen afterwards. The cart and trumpet for me.

This is all very well; but the trumpet is an instrument that grows on one; and sometimes my blasts have been so strident that even those who are most annoyed by them have mistaken the novelty of my shamelessness for novelty in my plays and opinions. Take, for instance [the play printed in the present volume] The Devil's Disciple. It does not contain a single even passably novel incident. Every old patron of the Adelphi pit would, were he not beglamored in a way presently to be explained, recognize the reading of the will, the oppressed orphan finding a protector, the arrest, the heroic sacrifice, the court martial, the scaffold, the reprieve at the last moment, as he recognizes beefsteak pudding on the bill of fare at his restaurant. Yet when the play was produced in 1897 in New York by Mr Richard Mansfield, with a success that proves either that the melodrama was built on very safe old lines, or that the American public is composed exclusively of men of genius, the critics, though one said one thing and another another as to the play's merits, yet all agreed that it was novel—*original*, as they put it—to the verge of audacious eccentricity.

Now this, if it applies to the incidents, plot, construction, and general professional and technical qualities of the play, is nonsense; for the truth is, I am in these matters a very old-fashioned playwright. When a good deal of the same talk, both hostile and friendly, was provoked by my last volume of plays, Mr Robert Buchanan, a dramatist who knows what I know and remembers what I remember of the history of the stage, pointed out that the stage tricks by which I gave the younger generation of playgoers an exquisite sense of quaint unexpectedness, had done duty years ago in Cool as a Cucumber, Used Up, and many forgotten farces and comedies of the Byron-Robertson school, in which the imperturbably impudent comedian, afterwards shelved by the reaction to brainless sentimentality, was a stock figure. It is always so more or less: the novelties of one generation are only the resuscitated fashions of the generation before last.

But the stage tricks of The Devil's Disciple are not, like some of those of Arms and the Man, the forgotten ones of the sixties, but the hackneyed ones of our own time. Why, then, were they not recognized? Partly, no doubt, because of my trumpet and cartwheel declamation. The critics were the victims of the long course of hypnotic suggestion by which G.B.S. the journalist manufactured an unconventional reputation for Bernard Shaw the author. In England as elsewhere the spontaneous recognition of really original work begins with a mere handful of people, and propagates itself so slowly that it has become a commonplace to say that genius, demanding bread, is given a stone after its possessor's death. The remedy for this is sedulous advertisement. Accordingly, I have advertized myself so well that I find myself, whilst still in middle life, almost as legendary a person as the Flying Dutchman. Critics, like other people, see what they look for, not what is actually before them. In my plays they look for my legendary qualities, and find originality and brilliancy in my most hackneyed claptraps. Were I to republish Buckstone's Wreck Ashore as my latest comedy, it would be hailed as a masterpiece of perverse paradox and scintillating satire. Not, of course, by the really able critics—for example, you, my friend, now reading this sentence. The illusion that makes *you* think me so original is far subtler than that. The Devil's Disciple has, in truth, a genuine novelty in it. Only, that novelty is not any invention of my own, but simply the novelty of the advanced thought of my day. As such, it will assuredly lose its gloss with the lapse of time, and leave The Devil's Disciple exposed as the threadbare popular melodrama it technically is.

Let me explain (for, as Mr A. B. Walkley has pointed out in his disquisitions on Frames of Mind, I am nothing if not explanatory). Dick Dudgeon, the devil's disciple, is a Puritan of the Puritans. He is brought up in a household where the Puritan religion has died, and become, in its corruption, an excuse for his mother's master passion of hatred in all its phases of cruelty and envy. This corruption has already been dramatized for us by Charles Dickens in his picture of the Clennam household in Little Dorrit: Mrs Dudgeon being a replica of Mrs Clennam with certain circumstantial variations, and perhaps a touch of the same author's Mrs Gargery in Great Expectations. In such a home the young Puritan finds himself starved of religion, which is the most clamorous need of his nature. With all his mother's indomitable selffulness, but with Pity instead of Hatred as his master passion, he pities the devil; takes his side; and champions him, like a true Covenanter, against the world. He thus becomes, like all genuinely religious men, a reprobate and an outcast. Once this is understood, the play becomes straightforwardly simple.

The Diabolonian position is new to the London playgoer of today, but not to lovers of serious literature. From Prometheus to the Wagnerian Siegfried, some enemy of the gods, unterrified champion of those oppressed by them, has always towered among the heroes of the loftiest poetry. Our newest idol, the Superman, celebrating the death of godhead, may be younger than the hills; but he is as old as the shepherds. Two and a half centuries ago our greatest English dramatizer of life, John Bunyan, ended one of his stories with the remark that there is a way to hell even from the gates of heaven, and so led us to the equally true proposition that there is a way to heaven even from the gates of hell. A century ago William Blake was, like Dick Dudgeon, an avowed Diabolonian: he called his angels devils and his devils angels. His devil is a Redeemer. Let those who have praised my originality in conceiving Dick Dudgeon's strange religion read Blake's Marriage of

Heaven and Hell, and I shall be fortunate if they do not rail at me for a plagiarist. But they need not go back to Blake and Bunyan. Have they not heard the recent fuss about Nietzsche and his Good and Evil Turned Inside Out? Mr Robert Buchanan has actually written a long poem of which the Devil is the merciful hero, which poem was in my hands before a word of The Devil's Disciple was written. There never was a play more certain to be written than The Devil's Disciple at the end of the nineteenth century. The age was visibly pregnant with it.

I grieve to have to add that my old friends and colleagues the London critics for the most part shewed no sort of connoisseurship either in Puritanism or in Diabolonianism when the play was performed for a few weeks at a suburban theatre (Kennington) in October 1899 by Mr Murray Carson. They took Mrs Dudgeon at her own valuation as a religious woman because she was detestably disagreeable. And they took Dick as a blackguard on her authority, because he was neither detestable nor disagreeable. But they presently found themselves in a dilemma. Why should a blackguard save another man's life, and that man no friend of his, at the risk of his own? Clearly, said the critics, because he is redeemed by love. All wicked heroes are, on the stage: that is the romantic metaphysic. Unfortunately for this explanation (which I do not profess to understand) it turned out in the third act that Dick was a Puritan in this respect also: a man impassioned only for saving grace, and not to be led or turned by wife or mother, Church or State, pride of life or lust of the flesh. In the lovely home of the courageous, affectionate, practical minister who marries a pretty wife twenty years younger than himself, and turns soldier in an instant to save the man who has saved him, Dick looks round and understands the charm and the peace and the sanctity, but knows that such material comforts are not for him. When the woman nursed in that atmosphere falls in love with him and concludes (like the critics, who somehow always agree with my sentimental heroines) that he risked his life for her sake, he tells her the obvious truth that he would have done as much for any stranger—that the law of his own nature, and no interest nor lust whatsoever, forbad him to cry out that the hangman's noose should be taken off his neck only to be put on another man's.

But then, said the critics, where is the motive? *Why* did Dick save Anderson? On the stage, it appears, people do things for reasons. Off the stage they dont: that is why your penny-in-the-slot heroes, who only work when you drop a motive into them, are so oppressively automatic and uninteresting. The saving of life at the risk of the saver's own is not a common thing: but modern populations are so vast that even the most uncommon things are recorded once a week or oftener. Not one of my critics but has seen a hundred times in his paper how some policeman or fireman or nursemaid has received a medal, or the compliments of a magistrate, or perhaps a public funeral, for risking his or her life to save another's. Has he ever seen it added that the saved was the husband of the woman the saver loved, or was that woman herself, or was even known to the saver as much as by sight? Never. When we want to read of the deeds that are done for love, whither do we turn? To the murder column; and there we are rarely disappointed.

Need I repeat that the theatre critic's professional routine so discourages any association between real life and the stage, that he soon loses the natural habit of referring to the one to explain the other? The critic who discovered a romantic motive for Dick's sacrifice was no mere literary dreamer, but a clever barrister. He pointed out that Dick Dudgeon clearly did adore Mrs Anderson; that it was for her sake that he offered his life to save her beloved husband; and that his explicit denial of his passion was the splendid mendacity of a gentleman whose respect for a married woman, and duty to her absent husband, sealed his passion-palpitating lips. From the moment that this fatally plausible explanation was launched, my play became my critic's play, not mine. Thenceforth Dick Dudgeon every night confirmed the critic by stealing behind Judith, and mutely attesting his passion by surreptitiously imprinting a heart-broken kiss on a stray lock of her hair whilst he uttered the barren denial. As for me, I was just then wandering about the streets of Constantinople, unaware of all these doings. When I returned all was over. My personal relations with the critic and the actor forbad me to curse them. I had not even the chance of publicly forgiving them. They meant well by me; but if they ever write a play, may I be there to explain![1]

SURREY, 1900.

[1] As I pass these pages through the press (September 1900), the critics of Yorkshire are struggling, as against some unholy fascination, with the apparition of Dick Dudgeon on their stage in the person of Forbes Robertson. "A finished scoundrel" is the description which one of them gives of Dick. This is worth recording as an example of the extent to which the moral sense remains dormant in people who are content with the customary formulas for respectable conduct.

THE DEVIL'S DISCIPLE
ACT I

At the most wretched hour between a black night and a wintry morning in the year 1777, Mrs Dudgeon, of New Hampshire, is sitting up in the kitchen and general dwelling room of her farm house on the outskirts of the town of Websterbridge. She is not a prepossessing woman. No woman looks her best after sitting up all night; and Mrs Dudgeon's face, even at its best, is grimly trenched by the channels into which the barren forms and observances of a dead Puritanism can pen a bitter temper and a fierce pride. She is an elderly matron who has worked hard and got nothing by it except dominion and detestation in her sordid home, and an unquestioned reputation for piety and respectability among her neighbors, to whom drink and debauchery are still so much more tempting than religion and rectitude, that they conceive goodness simply as self-denial. This conception is easily extended to others-denial, and finally generalized as covering anything disagreeable. So Mrs Dudgeon, being exceedingly disagreeable, is held to be exceedingly good. Short of flat felony, she enjoys complete license except for amiable weakness of any sort, and is consequently, without knowing it, the most licentious woman in the parish on the strength of never having broken the seventh commandment or missed a Sunday at the Presbyterian church.

The year 1777 is the one in which the passions roused by the breaking-off of the American colonies from England, more by their own weight than by their own will, boiled up to shooting point, the shooting being idealized to the English mind as suppression of rebellion and maintenance of British dominion, and to the American as defence of liberty, resistance to tyranny, and self-sacrifice on the altar of the Rights of Man. Into the merits of these idealizations it is not here necessary to inquire: suffice it to say, without prejudice, that they have convinced both Americans and English that the most highminded course for them to pursue is to kill as many of one

comparison drawn between 23
Mrs D to British

another as possible, and that military operations to that end are in full swing, morally supported by confident requests from the clergy of both sides for the blessing of God on their arms.

Under such circumstances many other women besides this disagreeable Mrs Dudgeon find themselves sitting up all night waiting for news. Like her, too, they fall asleep towards morning at the risk of nodding themselves into the kitchen fire. Mrs Dudgeon sleeps with a shawl over her head, and her feet on a broad fender of iron laths, the step of the domestic altar of the fireplace, with its huge hobs and boiler, and its hinged arm above the smoky mantelshelf for roasting. The plain kitchen table is opposite the fire, at her elbow, with a candle on it in a tin sconce. Her chair, like all the others in the room, is uncushioned and unpainted; but as it has a round railed back and a seat conventionally moulded to the sitter's curves, it is comparatively a chair of state. The room has three doors, one on the same side as the fireplace, near the corner, leading to the best bedroom; one, at the opposite end of the opposite wall, leading to the scullery and washhouse; and the housedoor, with its latch, heavy lock, and clumsy wooden bar, in the front wall, between the window in its middle and the corner next the bedroom door. Between the door and the window a rack of pegs suggests to the deductive observer that the men of the house are all away, as there are no coats or hats on them. On the other side of the window the clock hangs on a nail, with its white wooden dial, black iron weights, and brass pendulum. Between the clock and the corner, a big cupboard, locked, stands on a dwarf dresser full of common crockery.

On the side opposite the fireplace, between the door and the corner, a shamelessly ugly black horsehair sofa stands against the wall. An inspection of its stridulous surface shews that Mrs Dudgeon is not alone. A girl of sixteen or seventeen has fallen asleep on it. She is a wild, timid looking creature with black hair and tanned skin. Her frock, a scanty garment, is rent, weather-stained, berrystained, and by no means scrupulously clean. It hangs on her with a freedom which, taken with her brown legs and bare feet, suggests no great stock of underclothing.

24 house = basic

Suddenly there comes a tapping at the door, not loud enough to wake the sleepers. Then knocking, which disturbs Mrs Dudgeon a little. Finally the latch is tried, whereupon she springs up at once.

MRS DUDGEON [*threateningly*] Well, why dont you open the door? [*She sees that the girl is asleep, and immediately raises a clamor of heartfelt vexation*]. Well, dear, dear me! Now this is— [*shaking her*] wake up, wake up: do you hear?

THE GIRL [*sitting up*] What is it?

MRS DUDGEON. Wake up; and be ashamed of yourself, you unfeeling sinful girl, falling asleep like that, and your father hardly cold in his grave.

THE GIRL [*half asleep still*] I didnt mean to. I dropped off—

MRS DUDGEON [*cutting her short*] Oh yes, youve plenty of excuses, I daresay. Dropped off! [*Fiercely, as the knocking recommences*] Why dont you get up and let your uncle in? after me waiting up all night for him! [*She pushes her rudely off the sofa*]. There: I'll open the door: much good you are to wait up. Go and mend that fire a bit.

The girl, cowed and wretched, goes to the fire and puts a log on. Mrs Dudgeon unbars the door and opens it, letting into the stuffy kitchen a little of the freshness and a great deal of the chill of the dawn, also her second son Christy, a fattish, stupid, fair-haired, roundfaced man of about 22, muffled in a plaid shawl and grey overcoat. He hurries, shivering, to the fire, leaving Mrs Dudgeon to shut the door.

CHRISTY [*at the fire*] F—f—f! but it is cold. [*Seeing the girl, and staring lumpishly at her*] Why, who are you?

THE GIRL [*shyly*] Essie.

MRS DUDGEON. Oh, you may well ask. [*To Essie*] Go to your room, child, and lie down, since you havnt feeling enough to keep you awake. Your history isnt fit for your own ears to hear.

ESSIE. I—

MRS DUDGEON [*peremptorily*] Dont answer me, Miss; but shew your obedience by doing what I tell you. [*Essie, almost in tears, crosses the room to the door near the sofa].* And dont forget your prayers. *[Essie goes out].* She'd have gone to bed last night just as if nothing had happened if I'd let her.

CHRISTY *[phlegmatically]* Well, she cant be expected to feel Uncle Peter's death like one of the family.

MRS DUDGEON. What are you talking about, child? Isnt she his daughter—the punishment of his wickedness and shame? *[She assaults her chair by sitting down].*

CHRISTY *[staring]* Uncle Peter's daughter!

MRS DUDGEON. Why else should she be here? D'ye think Ive not had enough trouble and care put upon me bringing up my own girls, let alone you and your good-for-nothing brother, without having your uncle's bastards—

CHRISTY *[interrupting her with an apprehensive glance at the door by which Essie went out]* Sh! She may hear you.

MRS DUDGEON *[raising her voice]* Let her hear me. People who fear God dont fear to give the devil's work its right name. *[Christy, soullessly indifferent to the strife of Good and Evil, stares at the fire, warming himself].* Well, how long are you going to stare there like a stuck pig? What news have you for me?

CHRISTY *[taking off his hat and shawl and going to the rack to hang them up.]* The minister is to break the news to you. He'll be here presently.

MRS DUDGEON. Break what news?

CHRISTY *[standing on tiptoe, from boyish habit, to hang his hat up, though he is quite tall enough to reach the peg, and speaking with callous placidity, considering the nature of the announcement]* Father's dead too.

MRS DUDGEON *[stupent]* Your father!

CHRISTY *[sulkily, coming back to the fire and warming himself again, attending much more to the fire than to his mother]* Well, it's not my fault. When we got to Nevinstown we found him ill in bed. He didnt know us at first. The minister sat up with him and sent me away. He died in the night.

MRS DUGDEON *[bursting into dry angry tears]* Well, I do think this is hard on me—very hard on me. His brother, that was a disgrace to us all his life, gets hanged on the public gallows as a rebel; and your father, instead of staying at home where his duty was, with his own family, goes after him and dies, leaving everything on my shoulders. After sending this girl to me to take care of, too! [*She plucks her shawl vexedly over her ears*]. It's sinful, so it is: downright sinful.

CHRISTY [*with a slow, bovine cheerfulness, after a pause*] I think it's going to be a fine morning, after all.

MRS DUDGEON [*railing at him*] A fine morning! And your father newly dead! Wheres your feelings, child? *IRONIC, cos shes no feelings herself.*

CHRISTY [*obstinately*] Well, I didn't mean any harm. I suppose a man may make a remark about the weather even if his father's dead.

MRS DUDGEON [*bitterly*] A nice comfort my children are to me! One son a fool, and the other a lost sinner thats left his home to live with smugglers and gypsies and villains, the scum of the earth!

Someone knocks.

CHRISTY [*without moving*] Thats the minister.

MRS DUDGEON [*sharply*] Well, arnt you going to let Mr Anderson in?

Christy goes sheepishly to the door. Mrs Dudgeon buries her face in her hands, as it is her duty as a widow to be overcome with grief. Christy opens the door, and admits the minister, Anthony Anderson, a shrewd, genial, ready Presbyterian divine of about 50, with something of the authority of his profession in his bearing. But it is an altogether secular authority, sweetened by a conciliatory, sensible manner not at all suggestive of a quite thorough-going other-worldliness. He is a strong, healthy man too, with a thick sanguine neck; and his keen, cheerful mouth cuts into somewhat fleshy corners. No doubt an excellent parson, but still a man capable of making the most of this world, and perhaps a little apologetically conscious of getting on better with it than a sound Presbyterian ought.

ANDERSON [*to Christy, at the door, looking at Mrs Dudgeon whilst he takes off his cloak*] Have you told her?

27

CHRISTY. She made me. [*He shuts the door; yawns; and loafs across to the sofa, where he sits down and presently drops off to sleep*].

Anderson looks compassionately at Mrs Dudgeon. Then he hangs his cloak and hat on the rack. Mrs Dudgeon dries her eyes and looks up at him.

ANDERSON. Sister: the Lord has laid his hand very heavily upon you.

MRS DUDGEON [*with intensely recalcitrant resignation*] It's His will, I suppose; and I must bow to it. But I do think it hard. What call had Timothy to go to Springtown, and remind everybody that he belonged to a man that was being hanged?—and [*spitefully*] that deserved it, if ever a man did.

ANDERSON [*gently*] They were brothers, Mrs Dudgeon.

MRS DUDGEON. Timothy never acknowledged him as his brother after we were married: he had too much respect for me to insult me with such a brother. Would such a selfish wretch as Peter have come thirty miles to see Timothy hanged, do you think? Not thirty yards, not he. However, I must bear my cross as best I may: least said is soonest mended.

ANDERSON [*very grave, coming down to the fire to stand with his back to it*] Your eldest son was present at the execution, Mrs Dudgeon.

MRS DUDGEON [*disagreeably surprised*] Richard?

ANDERSON [*nodding*] Yes.

MRS DUDGEON [*vindictively*] Let it be a warning to him. He may end that way himself, the wicked, dissolute, godless—[*she suddenly stops; her voice fails; and she asks, with evident dread*] Did Timothy see him?

ANDERSON. Yes.

MRS DUDGEON [*holding her breath*] Well?

ANDERSON. He only saw him in the crowd: they did not speak. [*Mrs Dudgeon, greatly relieved, exhales the pent up breath and sits at her ease again*]. Your husband was greatly touched and impressed by his brother's awful death. [*Mrs Dudgeon sneers. Anderson breaks off to demand with some indignation*] Well, wasnt it only natural, Mrs Dudgeon? He softened towards his prodigal son in that moment. He sent for him to come to see him.

MRS DUDGEON [*her alarm renewed*] Sent for Richard!

ANDERSON. Yes; but Richard would not come. He sent his father a message; but I'm sorry to say it was a wicked message—an awful message.

MRS DUDGEON. What was it?

ANDERSON. That he would stand by his wicked uncle and stand against his good parents, in this world and the next.

MRS DUDGEON [*implacably*] He will be punished for it. He will be punished for it—in both worlds.

ANDERSON. That is not in our hands, Mrs Dudgeon.

MRS DUDGEON. Did I say it was, Mr Anderson? We are told that the wicked shall be punished. Why should we do our duty and keep God's law if there is to be no difference made between us and those who follow their own likings and dislikings, and make a jest of us and of their Maker's word?

ANDERSON. Well, Richard's earthly father has been merciful to him; and his heavenly judge is the father of us all.

MRS DUDGEON [*forgetting herself*] Richard's earthly father was a softheaded —

ANDERSON [*shocked*] Oh!

MRS DUDGEON [*with a touch of shame*] Well, I am Richard's mother. If I am against him who has any right to be for him? [*Trying to conciliate him*] Wont you sit down, Mr Anderson? I should have asked you before; but I'm so troubled.

ANDERSON. Thank you. [*He takes a chair from beside the fireplace, and turns it so that he can sit comfortably at the fire. When he is seated he adds, in the tone of a man who knows that he is opening a difficult subject*] Has Christy told you about the new will?

MRS DUDGEON [*all her fears returning*] The new will! Did Timothy—? [*She breaks off, gasping, unable to complete the question*].

ANDERSON. Yes. In his last hours he changed his mind.

MRS DUDGEON [*white with intense rage*] And you let him rob me?

ANDERSON. I had no power to prevent him giving what was his to his own son.

MRS DUDGEON. He had nothing of his own. His money was the money I brought him as my marriage portion. It was for me to deal with my own money and my own son. He dare not have done it if I had been with him; and well he knew it. That was why he stole away like a thief to take advantage of the law to rob me by making a new will behind my back. The more shame on you, Mr Anderson,—you, a minister of the gospel—to act as his accomplice in such a crime.

ANDERSON [*rising*] I will take no offence at what you say in the first bitterness of your grief.

MRS DUDGEON [*contemptuously*] Grief!

ANDERSON. Well, of your disappointment, if you can find it in your heart to think that the better word.

MRS DUDGEON. My heart! My heart! And since when, pray, have you begun to hold up our hearts as trustworthy guides for us?

ANDERSON [*rather guiltily*] I—er—

MRS DUDGEON [*vehemently*] Dont lie, Mr Anderson. We are told that the heart of man is deceitful above all things, and desperately wicked. My heart belonged, not to Timothy, but to that poor wretched brother of his that has just ended his days with a rope round his neck—aye, to Peter Dudgeon. You know it: old Eli Hawkins, the man to whose pulpit you succeeded, though you are not worthy to loose his shoe latchet, told it you when he gave over our souls into your charge. He warned me and strengthened me against my heart, and made me marry a Godfearing man—as he thought. What else but that discipline has made me the woman I am? And you, you, who followed your heart in your marriage, you talk to me of what I find in my heart. Go home to your pretty wife, man; and leave me to my prayers. [*She turns from him and leans with her elbows on the table, brooding over her wrongs and taking no further notice of him*].

ANDERSON [*willing enough to escape*] The Lord forbid that I should come between you and the source of all comfort! [*He goes to the rack for his coat and hat*].

MRS DUDGEON [*without looking at him*] The Lord will know what to forbid and what to allow without your help.

ANDERSON. And whom to forgive, I hope—Eli Hawkins and myself, if we have ever set up our preaching against His law. [*He fastens his cloak, and is now ready to go.*] Just one word—on necessary business, Mrs Dudgeon. There is the reading of the will to be gone through; and Richard has a right to be present. He is in the town; but he has the grace to say that he does not want to force himself in here.

MRS DUDGEON. He s h a l l come here. Does he expect us to leave his father's house for his convenience? Let them all come, and come quickly, and go quickly. They shall not make the will an excuse to shirk half their day's work. I shall be ready, never fear.

ANDERSON [*coming back a step or two*] Mrs Dudgeon: I used to have some little influence with you. When did I lose it?

MRS DUDGEON [*still without turning to him*] When you married for love. Now youre answered.

ANDERSON. Yes: I am answered. [*He goes out, musing*].

MRS DUDGEON [*to herself, thinking of her husband*] Thief! Thief!! [*She shakes herself angrily out of her chair; throws back the shawl from her head; and sets to work to prepare the room for the reading of the will, beginning by replacing Anderson's chair against the wall, and pushing back her own to the window. Then she calls, in her hard, driving, wrathful way*] Christy. [*No answer: he is fast asleep*]. Christy. [*She shakes him roughly*]. Get up out of that; and be ashamed of yourself—sleeping, and your father dead! [*She returns to the table; puts the candle on the mantelshelf; and takes from the table drawer a red table cloth which she spreads*].

CHRISTY [*rising reluctantly*] Well, do you suppose we are never going to sleep until we are out of mourning?

MRS DUDGEON. I want none of your sulks. Here: help me to set this table. [*They place the table in the middle of the room, with Christy's end towards the fireplace and Mrs Dudgeon's towards the sofa. Christy drops the table as soon as possible, and goes to the fire, leaving his mother to make the final adjustments of its position*]. We shall have the minister back here with the lawyer and all the family to read the will before you have done toasting yourself. Go and wake that girl; and then light the stove in the shed: you cant have your breakfast here. And mind you wash yourself, and make yourself fit to receive the company. [*She punctuates these orders by going to the cupboard; unlocking it; and producing a decanter of wine, which has no doubt stood there untouched since the last state occasion in the family, and some glasses, which she sets on the table. Also two green ware plates, on one of which she puts a barnbrack with a knife beside it. On the other she shakes some biscuits out of a tin, putting back one or two, and counting the rest*]. Now mind: there are ten biscuits there: let there be ten there when I come back after dressing myself. And keep your fingers off the raisins in that cake. And tell Essie the same. I suppose I can trust you to bring in the case of stuffed birds without breaking the glass? [*She replaces the tin in the cupboard, which she locks, pocketing the key carefully*].

CHRISTY [*lingering at the fire*] Youd better put the inkstand instead, for the lawyer.

MRS DUDGEON. Thats no answer to make to me, sir. Go and do as youre told. [*Christy turns sullenly to obey*]. Stop: take down that shutter before you go, and let the daylight in: you cant expect me to do all the heavy work of the house with a great lout like you idling about.

Christy takes the window bar out of its clamps, and puts it aside; then opens the shutter, shewing the grey morning. Mrs Dudgeon takes the sconce from the mantelshelf; blows out the candle; extinguishes the snuff by pinching it with her fingers, first licking them for the purpose; and replaces the sconce on the shelf.

CHRISTY [*looking through the window*] Heres the minister's wife.

MRS DUDGEON [*displeased*] What! Is she coming here?

CHRISTY. Yes.

MRS DUDGEON. What does she want troubling me at this hour, before I am properly dressed to receive people?

CHRISTY. You d better ask her.

MRS DUDGEON [*threateningly*] You d better keep a civil tongue in your head. [*He goes sulkily towards the door. She comes after him, plying him with instructions*]. Tell that girl to come to me as soon as she's had her breakfast. And tell her to make herself fit to be seen before the people. [*Christy goes out and slams the door in her face*]. Nice manners, that! [*Someone knocks at the house door: she turns and cries inhospitably*] Come in. [*Judith Anderson, the minister's wife, comes in. Judith is more than twenty years younger than her husband, though she will never be as young as he in vitality. She is pretty and proper and ladylike, and has been admired and petted into an opinion of herself sufficiently favorable to give her a self-assurance which serves her instead of strength. She has a pretty taste in dress, and in her face the pretty lines of a sentimental character formed by dreams. Even her little self-complacency is pretty, like a child's vanity. Rather a pathetic creature to any sympathetic observer who knows how rough a place the world is. One feels, on the whole, that Anderson might have chosen worse, and that she, needing protection, could not have chosen better*]. Oh, it's you, is it, Mrs Anderson?

JUDITH [*very politely—almost patronizingly*] Yes. Can I do anything for you, Mrs Dudgeon? Can I help to get the place ready before they come to read the will?

MRS DUDGEON [*stiffly*] Thank you, Mrs Anderson, my house is always ready for anyone to come into.

MRS ANDERSON [*with complacent amiability*] Yes, indeed it is. Perhaps you had rather I did not intrude on you just now.

MRS DUDGEON. Oh, one more or less will make no difference this morning, Mrs Anderson. Now that youre here, youd better stay. If you wouldnt mind shutting the door! [*Judith smiles, implying "How stupid of me?" and shuts it with an exasperating air of doing something pretty and becoming*]. Thats better. I must go and tidy myself a bit. I suppose you dont mind stopping here to receive anyone that comes until I'm ready.

JUDITH [*graciously giving her leave*] Oh yes, certainly. Leave that to me, Mrs Dudgeon; and take your time. [*She hangs her cloak and bonnet on the rack*].

MRS DUDGEON [*half sneering*] I thought that would be more in your way than getting the house ready. [*Essie comes back*]. Oh, here you are! [*Severely*] Come here: let me see you. [*Essie timidly goes to her. Mrs Dudgeon takes her roughly by the arm and pulls her round to inspect the results of her attempt to clean and tidy herself—results which shew little practice and less conviction*]. Mm! Thats what you call doing you hair properly, I suppose. It's easy to see what you are, and how you were brought up. [*She throws her arm away, and goes on, peremptorily*] Now you listen to me and do as youre told. You sit down there in the corner by the fire; and when the company comes dont dare to speak until youre spoken to. [*Essie creeps away to the fireplace*]. Your father's people had better see you and know youre there: theyre as much bound to keep you from starvation as I am. At any rate they might help. But let me have no chattering and making free with them, as if you were their equal. Do you hear?

ESSIE. Yes.

MRS DUDGEON. Well, then go and do as youre told. [*Essie sits down miserably on the corner of the fender farthest from the door*]. Never mind her, Mrs Anderson: you know who she is and what she is. If she gives you any trouble, just tell me; and I'll settle accounts with her. [*Mrs Dudgeon goes into the bedroom, shutting the door sharply behind her as if even it had to be made do its duty with a ruthless hand*].

JUDITH [*patronizing Essie, and arranging the cake and wine on the table more becomingly*] You must not mind if your aunt is strict with you. She is a very good woman, and desires your good too.

ESSIE [*in listless misery*] Yes.

JUDITH [*annoyed with Essie for her failure to be consoled and edified, and to appreciate the kindly condescension of the remark*] You are not going to be sullen, I hope, Essie.

ESSIE. No.

JUDITH. Thats a good girl! [*She places a couple of chairs at the table with their backs to the window, with a pleasant sense of being a more thoughtful housekeeper than Mrs Dudgeon*]. Do you know any of your father's relatives?

ESSIE. No. They wouldnt have anything to do with him: they were too religious. Father used to talk about Dick Dudgeon; but I never saw him.

JUDITH [*ostentatiously shocked*] Dick Dudgeon! Essie: do you wish to be a really respectable and grateful girl, and to make a place for yourself here by steady good conduct?

ESSIE [*very half-heartedly*] Yes.

JUDITH. Then you must never mention the name of Richard Dudgeon—never think even about him. He is a bad man.

ESSIE. What has he done?

JUDITH. You must not ask questions about him, Essie. You are too young to know what it is to be a bad man. But he is a smuggler; and he lives with gypsies; and he has no love for his mother and his family; and he wrestles and plays games on Sunday instead of going to church. Never let him into your presence, if you can help it, Essie; and try to keep yourself and all womanhood unspotted by contact with such men.

ESSIE. Yes.

JUDITH [*again displeased*] I am afraid you say Yes and No without thinking very deeply.

ESSIE. Yes. At least I mean—

JUDITH [*severely*] What do you mean?

ESSIE [*almost crying*] Only—my father was a smuggler; and— [*Someone knocks*].

JUDITH. They are beginning to come. Now remember your aunt's directions, Essie; and be a good girl. [*Christy comes back with the stand of stuffed birds under a glass case, and an inkstand, which he places on the table*]. Good morning, Mr Dudgeon. Will you open the door, please: the people have come.

CHRISTY. Good morning. [*He opens the house door*].

The morning is now fairly bright and warm; and Anderson, who is the first to enter, has left his cloak at home. He is accompanied by

*Lawyer Hawkins, a brisk, middleaged man in brown riding gaiters
and yellow breeches, looking as much squire as solicitor. He and
Anderson are allowed precedence as representing the learned professions. After them comes the family, headed by the senior uncle,
William Dudgeon, a large, shapeless man, bottle-nosed and evidently
no ascetic at table. His clothes are not the clothes, nor his anxious
wife the wife, of a prosperous man. The junior uncle, Titus Dudgeon,
is a wiry little terrier of a man, with an immense and visibly purse-
proud wife, both free from the cares of the William household.*

*Hawkins at once goes briskly to the table and takes the chair
nearest the sofa, Christy having left the inkstand there. He puts his
hat on the floor beside him, and produces the will. Uncle William
comes to the fire and stands on the hearth warming his coat tails,
leaving Mrs William derelict near the door. Uncle Titus, who is the
lady's man of the family, rescues her by giving her his disengaged
arm and bringing her to the sofa, where he sits down warmly between
his own lady and his brother's. Anderson hangs up his hat and waits
for a word with Judith.*

JUDITH. She will be here in a moment. Ask them to wait. [*She
taps at the bedroom door. Receiving an answer from within, she opens
it and passes through*].

ANDERSON [*taking his place at the table at the opposite end to
Hawkins*] .Our poor afflicted sister will be with us in a moment.
Are we all here?

CHRISTY [*at the house door, which he has just shut*] All except
Dick.

*The callousness with which Christy names the reprobate jars on
the moral sense of the family. Uncle William shakes his head slowly
and repeatedly. Mrs Titus catches her breath convulsively through
her nose. Her husband speaks.*

UNCLE TITUS. Well, I hope he will have the grace not to come.
I hope so.

*The Dudgeons all murmur assent, except Christy, who goes to the
window and posts himself there, looking out. Hawkins smiles secret-
ively as if he knew something that would change their tune if they*

36

knew it. Anderson is uneasy: the love of solemn family councils, especially funeral ones, is not in his nature. Judith appears at the bedroom door.

JUDITH [*with gentle impressiveness*] Friends, Mrs Dudgeon. [*She takes the chair from beside the fireplace; and places it for Mrs Dudgeon, who comes from the bedroom in black, with a clean handkerchief to her eyes. All rise, except Essie. Mrs Titus and Mrs William produce equally clean handkerchiefs and weep. It is an affecting moment*].

UNCLE WILLIAM. Would it comfort you, sister, if we were to offer up a prayer?

UNCLE TITUS. Or sing a hymn?

ANDERSON [*rather hastily*] I have been with our sister this morning already, friends. In our hearts we ask a blessing.

ALL [*except Essie*] Amen.

They all sit down, except Judith, who stands behind Mrs Dudgeon's chair.

JUDITH [*to Essie*] Essie: did you say Amen?

ESSIE [*scaredly*] No.

JUDITH. Then say it, like a good girl.

ESSIE. Amen.

UNCLE WILLIAM [*encouragingly*] Thats right: thats right. We know who you are; but we are willing to be kind to you if you are a good girl and deserve it. We are all equal before the Throne.

This republican sentiment does not please the women, who are convinced that the Throne is precisely the place where their superiority, often questioned in this world, will be recognized and rewarded.

CHRISTY [*at the window*] Heres Dick.

Anderson and Hawkins look round sociably. Essie, with a gleam of interest breaking through her misery, looks up. Christy grins and gapes expectantly at the door. The rest are petrified with the intensity of their sense of Virtue menaced with outrage by the approach of flaunting Vice. The reprobate appears in the doorway, graced beyond his alleged merits by the morning sunlight. He is certainly the best looking member of the family; but his expression is reckless and

37

sardonic, his manner defiant and satirical, his dress picturesquely careless. Only, his forehead and mouth betray an extraordinary steadfastness; and his eyes are the eyes of a fanatic.

RICHARD [*on the threshold, taking off his hat*] Ladies and gentlemen: your servant, your very humble servant. [*With this comprehensive insult, he throws his hat to Christy with a suddenness that makes him jump like a negligent wicket keeper, and comes into the middle of the room, where he turns and deliberately surveys the company*]. How happy you all look! how glad to see me! [*He turns towards Mrs Dudgeon's chair; and his lip rolls up horribly from his dog tooth as he meets her look of undisguised hatred*]. Well, mother: keeping up appearances as usual? thats right, thats right. [*Judith pointedly moves away from his neighborhood to the other side of the kitchen, holding her skirt instinctively as if to save it from contamination. Uncle Titus promptly marks his approval of her action by rising from the sofa, and placing a chair for her to sit down upon*]. What! Uncle William! I havnt seen you since you gave up drinking. [*Poor Uncle William, shamed, would protest; but Richard claps him heartily on his shoulder, adding*] you have given it up, havnt you? [*releasing him with a playful push*] of course you have: quite right too: you overdid it. [*He turns away from Uncle William and makes for the sofa*]. And now, where is that upright horsedealer Uncle Titus? Uncle Titus: come forth. [*He comes upon him holding the chair as Judith sits down*]. As usual, looking after the ladies!

UNCLE TITUS [*indignantly*] Be ashamed of yourself, sir—

RICHARD [*interrupting him and shaking his hand in spite of him*] I am: I am; but I am proud of my uncle—proud of all my relatives —[*again surveying them*] who could look at them and not be proud and joyful? [*Uncle Titus, overborne, resumes his seat on the sofa. Richard turns to the table*]. Ah, Mr Anderson, still at the good work, still shepherding them. Keep them up to the mark, minister, keep them up to the mark. Come! [*with a spring he seats himself on the table and takes up the decanter*] clink a glass with me, Pastor, for the sake of old times.

ANDERSON. You know, I think, Mr Dudgeon, that I do not drink before dinner.

RICHARD. You will, some day, Pastor: Uncle William used to drink before breakfast. Come: it will give your sermons unction. [*He smells the wine and makes a wry face*]. But do not begin on my mother's company sherry. I stole some when I was six years old; and I have been a temperate man ever since. [*He puts the decanter down and changes the subject*]. So I hear you are married, Pastor, and that your wife has a most ungodly allowance of good looks.

ANDERSON [*quietly indicating Judith*] Sir: you are in the presence of my wife. [*Judith rises and stands with stony propriety*].

RICHARD [*quickly slipping down from the table with instinctive good manners*] Your servant, madam: no offence. [*He looks at her earnestly*]. You deserve your reputation; but I'm sorry to see by your expression that youre a good woman. [*She looks shocked, and sits down amid a murmur of indignant sympathy from his relatives. Anderson, sensible enough to know that these demonstrations can only gratify and encourage a man who is deliberately trying to provoke them, remains perfectly goodhumored*]. All the same, Pastor, I respect you more than I did before. By the way, did I hear, or did I not, that our late lamented Uncle Peter, though unmarried, was a father?

UNCLE TITUS. He had only one irregular child, sir.

RICHARD. Only one! He thinks one a mere trifle! I blush for you, Uncle Titus.

ANDERSON. Mr Dudgeon: you are in the presence of your mother and her grief.

RICHARD. It touches me profoundly, Pastor. By the way, what has become of the irregular child?

ANDERSON [*pointing to Essie*] There, sir, listening to you.

RICHARD [*shocked into sincerity*] What! Why the devil didnt you tell me that before? Children suffer enough in this house without—[*He hurries remorsefully to Essie*]. Come, little cousin! never mind me: it was not meant to hurt you. [*She looks up gratefully at him. Her tearstained face affects him violently; and he bursts out, in a transport of wrath*] Who has been making her cry? Who has been ill-treating her? By God—

MRS DUDGEON [*rising and confronting him*] Silence your blasphemous tongue. I will bear no more of this. Leave my house.

RICHARD. How do you know it's your house until the will is read? [*They look at one another for a moment with intense hatred; and then she sinks, checkmated, into her chair. Richard goes boldly up past Anderson to the window, where he takes the railed chair in his hand*]. Ladies and gentlemen: as the eldest son of my late father, and the unworthy head of this household, I bid you welcome. By your leave, Minister Anderson: by your leave, Lawyer Hawkins. The head of the table for the head of the family. [*He places the chair at the table between the minister and the attorney; sits down between them; and addresses the assembly with a presidential air*]. We meet on a melancholy occasion: a father dead! an uncle actually hanged, and probably damned. [*He shakes his head deploringly. The relatives freeze with horror*]. Thats right: pull your longest faces [*his voice suddenly sweetens gravely as his glance lights on Essie*] provided only there is hope in the eyes of the child. [*Briskly*] Now then, Lawyer Hawkins; business, business. Get on with the will, man.

TITUS. Do not let yourself be ordered or hurried, Mr Hawkins.

HAWKINS [*very politely and willingly*] Mr Dudgeon means no offence, I feel sure. I will not keep you one second, Mr Dudgeon. Just while I get my glasses—[*he fumbles for them. The Dudgeons look at one another with misgiving*].

RICHARD. Aha! They notice your civility, Mr Hawkins. They are prepared for the worst. A glass of wine to clear your voice before you begin. [*He pours out one for him and hands it; then pours one for himself*].

HAWKINS. Thank you, Mr Dudgeon, Your good health, sir.

RICHARD. Yours, sir. [*With the glass half way to his lips, he checks himself, giving a dubious glance at the wine, and adds, with quaint intensity*] Will anyone oblige me with a glass of water?

Essie, who has been hanging on his every word and movement,

40

rises stealthily and slips out behind Mrs Dudgeon through the bedroom door, returning presently with a jug and going out of the house as quietly as possible.

HAWKINS. The will is not exactly in proper legal phraseology.

RICHARD. No: my father died without the consolations of the law.

HAWKINS. Good again, Mr Dudgeon, good again. [*Preparing to read*] Are you ready, sir?

RICHARD. Ready, aye ready. For what we are about to receive, may the Lord make us truly thankful. Go ahead.

HAWKINS [*reading*] "This is the last will and testament of me Timothy Dudgeon on my deathbed at Nevinstown on the road from Springtown to Websterbridge on this twenty-fourth day of September, one thousand seven hundred and seventy seven. I hereby revoke all former wills made by me and declare that I am of sound mind and know well what I am doing and that this is my real will according to my own wish and affections."

RICHARD [*glancing at his mother*] Aha!

HAWKINS [*shaking his head*] Bad phraseology, sir, wrong phraseology. "I give and bequeath a hundred pounds to my younger son Christopher Dudgeon, fifty pounds to be paid to him on the day of his marriage to Sarah Wilkins if she will have him, and ten pounds on the birth of each of his children up to the number of five."

RICHARD. How if she wont have him?

CHRISTY. She will if I have fifty pounds.

RICHARD. Good, my brother. Proceed.

HAWKINS. "I give and bequeath to my wife Annie Dudgeon, born Annie Primrose"—you see he did not know the law, Mr Dudgeon: your mother was not born Annie: she was christened so—"an annuity of fifty-two pounds a year for life [*Mrs Dudgeon, with all eyes on her, holds herself convulsively rigid*] to be paid out of the interest on her own money"—theres a way to put it, Mr Dudgeon! Her own money!

MRS DUDGEON. A very good way to put God's truth. It was every penny my own. Fifty-two pounds a year!

HAWKINS. "And I recommend her for her goodness and piety to the forgiving care of her children, having stood between them and her as far as I could to the best of my ability."

MRS DUDGEON. And this is my reward! [*Raging inwardly*] You know what I think, Mr Anderson: you know the word I gave to it.

ANDERSON. It cannot be helped, Mrs Dudgeon. We must take what comes to us. [*To Hawkins*]. Go on, sir.

HAWKINS. "I give and bequeath my house at Websterbridge with the land belonging to it and all the rest of my property soever to my eldest son and heir, Richard Dudgeon."

RICHARD. Oho! The fatted calf, Minister, the fatted calf.

HAWKINS. "On these conditions——"

RICHARD. The devil! Are there conditions?

HAWKINS. "To wit: first, that he shall not let my brother Peter's natural child starve or be driven by want to an evil life."

RICHARD [*emphatically, striking his fist on the table*] Agreed.

Mrs Dudgeon, turning to look malignantly at Essie, misses her and looks quickly round to see where she has moved to; then, seeing that she has left the room without leave, closes her lips vengefully.

HAWKINS. "Second, that he shall be a good friend to my old horse Jim"—[*again shaking his head*] he should have written James, sir.

RICHARD. James shall live in clover. Go on.

HAWKINS.—"and keep my deaf farm labourer Prodger Feston in his service."

RICHARD. Prodger Feston shall get drunk every Saturday.

HAWKINS. "Third, that he make Christy a present on his marriage out of the ornaments in the best room."

RICHARD [*holding up the stuffed birds*] Here you are, Christy.

CHRISTY [*disappointed*] I'd rather have the china peacocks.

RICHARD. You shall have both. [*Christy is greatly pleased*]. Go on.

HAWKINS. "Fourthly and lastly, that he try to live at peace with his mother as far as she will consent to it."

RICHARD [*dubiously*] Hm! Anything more, Mr Hawkins?

HAWKINS [*solemnly*] "Finally I give and bequeath my soul into my Maker's hands, humbly asking forgiveness for all my sins and mistakes, and hoping that He will so guide my son that it may not be said that I have done wrong in trusting to him rather than to others in the perplexity of my last hour in this strange place."

ANDERSON. Amen.

THE UNCLES AND AUNTS. Amen.

RICHARD. My mother does not say Amen.

MRS DUDGEON [*rising, unable to give up her property without a struggle*] Mr Hawkins: is that a proper will? Remember, I have his rightful, legal will, drawn up by yourself, leaving all to me.

HAWKINS. This is a very wrongly and irregularly worded will, Mrs Dudgeon: though [*turning politely to Richard*] it contains in my judgment an excellent disposal of his property.

ANDERSON [*interposing before Mrs Dudgeon can retort*] That is not what you are asked, Mr Hawkins. Is it a legal will?

HAWKINS. The courts will sustain it against the other.

ANDERSON. But why, if the other is more lawfully worded?

HAWKINS. Because, sir, the courts will sustain the claim of a man—and that man the eldest son—against any woman, if they can. I warned you, Mrs Dudgeon, when you got me to draw that other will, that it was not a wise will, and that though you might make him sign it, he would never be easy until he revoked it. But you wouldnt take advice; and now Mr Richard is cock of the walk. [*He takes his hat from the floor; rises; and begins pocketing his papers and spectacles*].

This is the signal for the breaking-up of the party. Anderson takes his hat from the rack and joins Uncle William at the fire. Titus fetches Judith her things from the rack. The three on the sofa rise and chat with Hawkins. Mrs Dudgeon, now an intruder in her own house, stands inert, crushed by the weight of the law on women, accepting it, as she has been trained to accept all monstrous calamities, as proofs of the greatness of the power that inflicts them, and of her own worm-like insignificance. For at this time, remember, Mary Wollstonecraft is as yet only a girl of eighteen, and her Vindication of the Rights of

Women is still fourteen years off. Mrs Dudgeon is rescued from her apathy by Essie, who comes back with the jug full of water. She is taking it to Richard when Mrs Dudgeon stops her.

MRS DUDGEON [*threatening her*] Where have you been? [*Essie, appalled, tries to answer, but cannot*]. How dare you go out by yourself after the orders I gave you?

ESSIE. He asked for a drink—[*she stops, her tongue cleaving to her palate with terror*].

JUDITH [*with gentler severity*] Who asked for a drink? [*Essie, speechless, points to Richard*].

RICHARD. What! I!

JUDITH [*shocked*] Oh Essie, Essie!

RICHARD. I believe I did. [*He takes a glass and holds it to Essie to be filled. Her hand shakes*]. What! afraid of me?

ESSIE [*quickly*] No. I—[*She pours out the water*].

RICHARD [*tasting it*] Ah, youve been up the street to the market gate spring to get that. [*He takes a draught*]. Delicious! Thank you. [*Unfortunately, at this moment he chances to catch sight of Judith's face, which expresses the most prudish disapproval of his evident attraction for Essie, who is devouring him with her grateful eyes. His mocking expression returns instantly. He puts down the glass; deliberately winds his arm round Essie's shoulders; and brings her into the middle of the company. Mrs Dudgeon being in Essie's way as they come past the table, he says*] By your leave, mother [*and compels her to make way for them*]. What do they call you? Bessie?

ESSIE. Essie.

RICHARD. Essie, to be sure. Are you a good girl, Essie?

ESSIE [*greatly disappointed that he, of all people, should begin at her in this way*] Yes. [*She looks doubtfully at Judith*]. I think so. I mean I—I hope so.

RICHARD. Essie: did you ever hear of a person called the devil?

ANDERSON [*revolted*] Shame on you, sir, with a mere child—

RICHARD. By your leave, Minister: I do not interfere with your sermons: do not you interrupt mine. [*To Essie*] Do you know what they call me, Essie?

ESSIE. Dick.

RICHARD [*amused: patting her on the shoulder*] Yes, Dick; but something else too. They call me the Devil's Disciple.

ESSIE. Why do you let them?

RICHARD [*seriously*] Because it's true. I was brought up in the other service; but I knew from the first that the Devil was my natural master and captain and friend. I saw that he was in the right, and that the world cringed to his conqueror only through fear. I prayed secretly to him: and he comforted me, and saved me from having my spirit broken in this house of children's tears. I promised him my soul, and swore an oath that I would stand up for him in this world and stand by him in the next. [*Solemnly*] That promise and that oath made a man of me. From this day this house is his home; and no child shall cry in it: this hearth is his altar; and no soul shall ever cower over it in the dark evenings and be afraid. Now [*turning forcibly on the rest*] which of you good men will take this child and rescue her from the house of the devil?

JUDITH [*coming to Essie and throwing a protecting arm about her*] I will. You should be burnt alive.

ESSIE. But I dont want to. [*She shrinks back, leaving Richard and Judith face to face*].

RICHARD [*to Judith*] Actually doesnt want to, most virtuous lady!

UNCLE TITUS. Have a care, Richard Dudgeon. The law—

RICHARD [*turning threateningly on him*] Have a care, you. In an hour from this there will be no law here but martial law. I passed the soldiers within six miles on my way here: before noon Major Swindon's gallows for rebels will be up in the market place.

ANDERSON [*calmly*] What have we to fear from that, sir?

RICHARD. More than you think. He hanged the wrong man at Springtown: he thought Uncle Peter was respectable, because the Dudgeons had a good name. But his next example will be the best man in the town to whom he can bring home a rebellious word. Well, we're all rebels; and you know it.

ALL THE MEN [*except Anderson*] No, no, no!

RICHARD. Yes, you are. You havnt damned King George up hill and down dale as I have; but youve prayed for his defeat; and you, Anthony Anderson, have conducted the service, and sold your family bible to buy a pair of pistols. They maynt hang me, perhaps; because the moral effect of the Devil's Disciple dancing on nothing wouldnt help them. But a minister! [*Judith, dismayed, clings to Anderson*] or a lawyer! [*Hawkins smiles like a man able to take care of himself*] or an upright horsedealer! [*Uncle Titus snarls at him in rage and terror*] or a reformed drunkard! [*Uncle William, utterly unnerved, moans and wobbles with fear*] eh? Would that shew that King George meant business—ha?

ANDERSON [*perfectly self-possessed*] Come, my dear: he is only trying to frighten you. There is no danger. [*He takes her out of the house. The rest crowd to the door to follow him, except Essie, who remains near Richard*].

RICHARD [*boisterously derisive*] Now then: how many of you will stay with me; run up the American flag on the devil's house; and make a fight for freedom? [*They scramble out, Christy among them, hustling one another in their haste*] Ha ha! Long live the devil! [*To Mrs Dudgeon, who is following them*] What, mother! Are you off too?

MRS DUDGEON [*deadly pale, with her hand on her heart as if she had received a deathblow*] My curse on you! My dying curse! [*She goes out*].

RICHARD [*calling after her*] It will bring me luck. Ha ha ha!

ESSIE [*anxiously*] Maynt I stay?

RICHARD [*turning to her*] What! Have they forgotten to save your soul in their anxiety about their own bodies? Oh yes: you may stay. [*He turns excitedly away again and shakes his fist after them. His left fist, also clenched, hangs down. Essie seizes it and kisses it, her tears falling on it. He starts and looks at it*]. Tears! The devil's baptism! [*She falls on her knees, sobbing. He stoops goodnaturedly to raise her, saying*] Oh yes, you may cry that way, Essie, if you like.

ACT II

Minister Anderson's house is in the main street of Webster-bridge, not far from the town hall. To the eye of the eighteenth century New Englander, it is much grander than the plain farmhouse of the Dudgeons; but it is so plain itself that a modern house agent would let both at about the same rent. The chief dwelling room has the same sort of kitchen fireplace, with boiler, toaster hanging on the bars, movable iron griddle socketed to the hob, hook above for roasting, and broad fender, on which stand a kettle and a plate of buttered toast. The door, between the fireplace and the corner, has neither panels, fingerplates nor handles: it is made of plain boards, and fastens with a latch. The table is a kitchen table, with a treacle colored cover of American cloth, chapped at the corners by draping. The tea service on it consists of two thick cups and saucers of the plainest ware, with milk jug and bowl to match, each large enough to contain nearly a quart, on a black japanned tray, and, in the middle of the table, a wooden trencher with a big loaf upon it, and a square half pound block of butter in a crock. The big oak press facing the fire from the opposite side of the room, is for use and storage, not for ornament; and the minister's house coat hangs on a peg from its door, shewing that he is out, for when he is in, it is his best coat that hangs there. His big riding boots stand beside the press, evidently in their usual place, and rather proud of themselves. In fact, the evolution of the minister's kitchen, dining room and drawing room into three separate apartments has not yet taken place; and so, from the point of view of our pampered period, he is no better off than the Dudgeons.

But there is a difference, for all that. To begin with, Mrs Anderson is a pleasanter person to live with than Mrs Dudgeon. To which Mrs Dudgeon would at once reply, with reason, that Mrs Anderson has no children to look after; no poultry, pigs nor cattle; a steady and sufficient income not directly dependent on harvests and prices at fairs; an affectionate husband who is a tower of strength to her: in short, that life is as easy at the minister's house as it is hard at the farm. This is true; but to explain a fact is not to alter it; and however little credit Mrs Anderson may deserve for making her home happier, she has certainly succeeded in doing it. The outward and visible signs of her superior social pretensions are, a drugget on the floor, a plaster ceiling between the timbers, and chairs which, though not upholstered, are stained and polished. The fine arts are represented by a mezzotint portrait of some Presbyterian divine, a copperplate of Raphael's St Paul preaching at Athens, a rococo presentation clock on the mantel-shelf, flanked by a couple of miniatures, a pair of crockery dogs with baskets in their mouths, and, at the corners, two large cowrie shells. A pretty feature of the room is the low wide latticed window, nearly its whole width, with little red curtains running on a rod half way up it to serve as a blind. There is no sofa; but one of the seats, standing near the press, has a railed back and is long enough to accommodate two people easily. On the whole, it is rather the sort of room that the nineteenth century has ended in struggling to get back to under the leadership of Mr Philip Webb and his disciples in domestic archi-tecture, though no genteel clergyman would have tolerated it fifty years ago.

The evening has closed in; and the room is dark except for the cosy firelight and the dim oil lamps seen through the window in the wet street where there is a quiet, steady, warm, windless downpour of rain. As the town clock strikes the quarter, Judith comes in with a couple of candles in earthenware candlesticks, and sets them on the table. Her self-conscious airs of the morning are gone: she is anxious and frightened. She goes to the window and peers into the street. The first thing she sees there is her husband, hurrying home through the rain. She gives a little gasp of relief, not very far removed from a sob, and turns to the door. Anderson comes in, wrapped in a very wet cloak.

JUDITH [*running to him*] Oh, here you are at last, at last! [*She attempts to embrace him*].

ANDERSON [*keeping her off*] Take care, my love: I'm wet. Wait till I get my cloak off. [*He places a chair with its back to the fire;*

hangs his cloak on it to dry; shakes the rain from his hat and puts it on the fender; and at last turns with his hands outstretched to Judith]. Now! [*She flies into his arms*]. I am not late, am I? The town clock struck the quarter as I came in at the front door. And the town clock is always fast.

JUDITH. I'm sure it's slow this evening. I'm so glad youre back.

ANDERSON [*taking her more closely in his arms*] Anxious, my dear?

JUDITH. A little.

ANDERSON. Why, youve been crying.

JUDITH. Only a little. Never mind: it's all over now. [*A bugle call is heard in the distance. She starts in terror and retreats to the long seat, listening.*] Whats that?

ANDERSON [*following her tenderly to the seat and making her sit down with him*] Only King George, my dear. He's returning to barracks, or having his roll called, or getting ready for tea, or booting or saddling or something. Soldiers dont ring the bell or call over the banisters when they want anything: they send a boy out with a bugle to disturb the whole town.

JUDITH. Do you think there is really any danger?

ANDERSON. Not the least in the world.

JUDITH. You say that to comfort me, not because you believe it.

ANDERSON. My dear: in this world there is always danger for those who are afraid of it. Theres a danger that the house will catch fire in the night; but we shant sleep any the less soundly for that.

JUDITH. Yes, I know what you always say; and youre quite right. Oh, quite right: I know it. But—I suppose I'm not brave: thats all. My heart shrinks every time I think of the soldiers.

ANDERSON. Never mind that, dear: bravery is none the worse for costing a little pain.

JUDITH. Yes, I suppose so, [*Embracing him again*] Oh how brave you are, my dear! [*With tears in her eyes*] Well, I'll be brave too: you shant be ashamed of your wife.

ANDERSON. Thats right. Now you make me happy. Well, well!

[*He rises and goes cheerily to the fire to dry his shoes*]. I called on Richard Dudgeon on my way back; but he wasnt in.

JUDITH [*rising in consternation*] You called on that man!

ANDERSON [*reassuring her*] Oh, nothing happened, dearie. He was out.

JUDITH [*almost in tears, as if the visit were a personal humiliation to her*] But why did you go there?

ANDERSON [*gravely*] Well, it is all the talk that Major Swindon is going to do what he did in Springtown—make an example of some notorious rebel, as he calls us. He pounced on Peter Dudgeon as the worst character there; and it is the general belief that he will pounce on Richard as the worst here.

JUDITH. But Richard said—

ANDERSON [*goodhumoredly cutting her short*] Pooh! Richard said! He said what he thought would frighten you and frighten me, my dear. He said what perhaps (God forgive him!) he would like to believe. It's a terrible thing to think of what death must mean for a man like that. I felt that I must warn him. I left a message for him.

JUDITH [*querulously*] What message?

ANDERSON. Only that I should be glad to see him for a moment on a matter of importance to himself, and that if he would look in here when he was passing he would be welcome.

JUDITH [*aghast*] You asked that man to come here!

ANDERSON. I did.

JUDITH [*sinking on the seat and clasping her hands*] I hope he wont come! Oh, I pray that he may not come!

ANDERSON. Why? Dont you want him to be warned?

JUDITH. He must know his danger. Oh, Tony, is it wrong to hate a blasphemer and a villain? I do hate him. I cant get him out of my mind: I know he will bring harm with him. He insulted you: he insulted me: he insulted his mother.

ANDERSON [*quaintly*] Well, dear, lets forgive him; and then it wont matter.

JUDITH. Oh, I know it's wrong to hate anybody; but—

ANDERSON [*going over to her with humorous tenderness*] Come, dear, youre not so wicked as you think. The worst sin towards our fellow creatures is not to hate them, but to be indifferent to them; thats the essence of inhumanity. After all, my dear, if you watch people carefully, youll be surprised to find how like hate is to love. [*She starts, strangely touched—even appalled. He is amused at her*]. Yes: I'm quite in earnest. Think of how some of our married friends worry one another, tax one another, are jealous of one another, cant bear to let one another out of sight for a day, are more like jailers and slave-owners than lovers. Think of those very same people with their enemies, scrupulous, lofty, self-respecting, determined to be independent of one another, careful of how they speak of one another—pooh! havnt you often thought that if they only knew it, they were better friends to their enemies than to their own husbands and wives? Come: depend on it, my dear, you are really fonder of Richard than you are of me, if you only knew it. Eh ?

JUDITH. Oh, dont say that: dont say that, Tony, even in jest. You dont know what a horrible feeling it gives me.

ANDERSON [*laughing*] Well, well: never mind, pet. He's a bad man; and you hate him as he deserves. And youre going to make the tea, arnt you?

JUDITH [*remorsefully*] Oh yes, I forgot. Ive been keeping you waiting all this time. [*She goes to the fire and puts on the kettle*].

ANDERSON [*going to the press and taking his coat off*] Have you stitched up the shoulder of my old coat?

JUDITH. Yes, dear. [*She goes to the table, and sets about putting the tea into the teapot from the caddy*].

ANDERSON [*as he changes his coat for the older one hanging on the press, and replaces it by the one he has just taken off*] Did anyone call when I was out?

JUDITH. No, only—[*Someone knocks at the door. With a start which betrays her intense nervousness, she retreats to the farther end of the table with the tea caddy and spoon in her hands exclaiming*] Who's that?

ANDERSON [*going to her and patting her encouragingly on the shoulder*] All right, pet, all right. He wont eat you, whoever he is. [*She tries to smile, and nearly makes herself cry. He goes to the door and opens it. Richard is there, without overcoat or cloak*]. You might have raised the latch and come in, Mr Dudgeon. Nobody stands on much ceremony with us. [*Hospitably*] Come in. [*Richard comes in carelessly and stands at the table, looking round the room with a slight pucker of his nose at the mezzotinted divine on the wall. Judith keeps her eyes on the tea caddy*]. Is it still raining? [*He shuts the door*].

RICHARD. Raining like the very [*his eye catches Judith's as she looks quickly and haughtily up*]—I beg your pardon; but [*shewing that his coat is wet*] you see—!

ANDERSON. Take it off, sir; and let it hang before the fire a while: my wife will excuse your shirtsleeves. Judith: put in another spoonful of tea for Mr Dudgeon.

RICHARD [*eyeing him cynically*] The magic of property, Pastor! Are even you civil to me now that I have succeeded to my father's estate?

Judith throws down the spoon indignantly.

ANDERSON [*quite unruffled, and helping Richard off with his coat*] I think, sir, that since you accept my hospitality, you cannot have so bad an opinion of it. Sit down. [*With the coat in his hand, he points to the railed seat. Richard, in his shirtsleeves, looks at him half quarrelsomely for a moment; then, with a nod, acknowledges that the minister has got the better of him, and sits down on the seat. Anderson pushes his cloak into a heap on the seat of the chair at the fire, and hangs Richard's coat on the back in its place*].

RICHARD. I come, sir, on your own invitation. You left word you had something important to tell me.

ANDERSON. I have a warning which it is my duty to give you.

RICHARD [*quickly rising*] You want to preach to me. Excuse me: I prefer a walk in the rain [*he makes for his coat*].

ANDERSON [*stopping him*] Dont be alarmed, sir: I am no great preacher. You are quite safe. [*Richard smiles in spite of himself. His glance softens: he even makes a gesture of excuse. Anderson, seeing that he has tamed him, now addresses him earnestly*] Mr Dudgeon: you are in danger in this town.

RICHARD. What danger?

ANDERSON. Your uncle's danger. Major Swindon's gallows.

RICHARD. It is you who are in danger. I warned you—

ANDERSON [*interrupting him goodhumoredly but authoritatively*] Yes, yes, Mr Dudgeon; but they do not think so in the town. And even if I were in danger, I have duties here which I must not forsake. But you are a free man. Why should you run any risk?

RICHARD. Do you think I should be any great loss, Minister?

ANDERSON. I think that a man's life is worth saving, whoever it belongs to. [*Richard makes him an ironical bow. Anderson returns the bow humorously*] Come: youll have a cup of tea, to prevent you catching cold?

RICHARD. I observe that Mrs Anderson is not quite so pressing as you are, Pastor.

JUDITH [*almost stifled with resentment, which she has been expecting her husband to share and express for her at every insult of Richard's*] You are welcome for my husband's sake. [*She brings the teapot to the fireplace and sets it on the hob*].

RICHARD. I know I am not welcome for my own, madam. [*He rises*]. But I think I will not break bread here, Minister.

ANDERSON [*cheerily*] Give me a good reason for that.

RICHARD. Because there is something in you that I respect, and that makes me desire to have you for my enemy.

ANDERSON. Thats well said. On these terms, sir, I will accept your enmity or any man's. Judith: Mr Dudgeon will stay to tea. Sit down: it will take a few minutes to draw by the fire. [*Richard glances at him with a troubled face; then sits down with his head bent, to hide a convulsive swelling of his throat*]. I was just saying to my wife, Mr Dudgeon, that enmity—[*She grasps his hand and looks imploringly at him, doing both with an intensity that checks him at once*]. Well, well, I mustnt tell you, I see; but it was nothing that need leave us worse friend—enemies, I mean. Judith is a great enemy of yours.

RICHARD. If all my enemies were like Mrs Anderson, I should be the best Christian in America.

ANDERSON [*gratified, patting her hand*] You hear that, Judith? Mr Dudgeon knows how to turn a compliment.

The latch is lifted from without.

JUDITH [*staring*] Who is that?

Christy comes in.

CHRISTY [*stopping and staring at Richard*] Oh, are you here?

RICHARD. Yes. Begone, you fool: Mrs Anderson doesnt want the whole family to tea at once.

CHRISTY [*coming further in*] Mother's very ill.

RICHARD. Well, does she want to see me?

CHRISTY. No.

RICHARD. I thought not.

CHRISTY. She wants to see the minister—at once.

JUDITH [*to Anderson*] Oh, not before youve had some tea.

ANDERSON. I shall enjoy it more when I come back, dear. [*He is about to take up his cloak*].

CHRISTY. The rain's over.

ANDERSON [*dropping the cloak and picking up his hat from the fender*] Where is your mother, Christy?

CHRISTY. At Uncle Titus's.

ANDERSON. Have you fetched the doctor?

CHRISTY. No: she didnt tell me to.

ANDERSON. Go on there at once: I'll overtake you on his door-step. [*Christy turns to go*]. Wait a moment. Your brother must be anxious to know the particulars.

RICHARD. Psha! not I: he doesnt know; and I dont care. [*Violently*] Be off, you oaf. [*Christy runs out. Richard adds, a little shamefacedly*] We shall know soon enough.

ANDERSON. Well, perhaps you will let me bring you the news myself. Judith: will you give Mr Dudgeon his tea, and keep him here until I return.

JUDITH [*white and trembling*] Must I—

ANDERSON [*taking her hands and interrupting her to cover her agitation*] My dear: I can depend on you?

JUDITH [*with a piteous effort to be worthy of his trust*] Yes.

ANDERSON [*pressing her hand against his cheek*] You will not mind two old people like us, Mr Dudgeon. [*Going*] I shall not say good evening: you will be here when I come back. [*He goes out*].

They watch him pass the window, and then look at each other dumbly, quite disconcerted. Richard, noting the quiver of her lips, is the first to pull himself together.

RICHARD. Mrs Anderson: I am perfectly aware of the nature of your sentiments towards me. I shall not intrude on you. Good evening. [*Again he starts for the fireplace to get his coat*].

JUDITH [*getting between him and the coat*] No, no. Dont go: please dont go.

RICHARD [*roughly*] Why? You dont want me here.

JUDITH. Yes, I—[*Wringing her hands in despair*] Oh, if I tell you the truth, you will use it to torment me.

RICHARD [*indignantly*] Torment! What right have you to say that? Do you expect me to stay after that?

JUDITH. I want you to stay; but [*suddenly raging at him like an angry child*] it is not because I like you.

RICHARD. Indeed!

JUDITH. Yes: I had rather you did go than mistake me about that. I hate and dread you; and my husband knows it. If you are not here when he comes back, he will believe that I disobeyed him and drove you away.

RICHARD [*ironically*] Whereas, of course, you have really been so kind and hospitable and charming to me that I only want to go away out of mere contrariness, eh?

Judith, unable to bear it, sinks on the chair and bursts into tears.

RICHARD. Stop, stop, stop, I tell you. Dont do that. [*Putting his hand to his breast as if to a wound*] He wrung my heart by being a man. Need you tear it by being a woman? Has he not raised you above my insults, like himself? [*She stops crying, and recovers herself somewhat, looking at him with a scared curiosity*]. There: thats right. [*Sympathetically*] Youre better now, arnt you? [*He puts his hand encouragingly on her shoulder. She instantly rises haughtily, and stares at him defiantly. He at once drops into his usual sardonic tone*]. Ah, thats better. You are yourself again: so is Richard. Well, shall we go to tea like a quiet respectable couple, and wait for your husband's return?

JUDITH [*rather ashamed of herself*] If you please. I—I am sorry to have been so foolish. [*She stoops to take up the plate of toast from the fender*].

RICHARD. I am sorry, for your sake, that I am—what I am. Allow me. [*He takes the plate from her and goes with it to the table*].

JUDITH [*following with the teapot*] Will you sit down? [*He sits down at the end of the table nearest the press. There is a plate and knife laid there. The other plate is laid near it: but Judith stays at the opposite end of the table, next the fire, and takes her place there, drawing the tray towards her*]. Do you take sugar?

RICHARD. No: but plenty of milk. Let me give you some toast. [*He puts some on the second plate, and hands it to her, with the knife. The action shews quickly how well he knows that she has avoided her usual place so as to be as far from him as possible*].

JUDITH [*consciously*] Thanks. [*She gives him his tea*]. Wont you help yourself?

RICHARD. Thanks. [*He puts a piece of toast on his own plate; and she pours out tea for herself*].

JUDITH [*observing that he tastes nothing*] Dont you like it? You are not eating anything.

RICHARD. Neither are you.

JUDITH [*nervously*] I never care much for my tea. Please dont mind me.

RICHARD [*looking dreamily round*] I am thinking. It is all so strange to me. I can see the beauty and peace of this home: I think I have never been more at rest in my life than at this moment; and yet I know quite well I could never live here. It's not in my nature, I suppose, to be domesticated. But it's very beautiful: it's almost holy. [*He muses a moment, and then laughs softly*].

JUDITH [*quickly*] Why do you laugh?

RICHARD. I was thinking that if any stranger came in here now, he would take us for man and wife.

JUDITH [*taking offence*] You mean, I suppose, that you are more my age than he is.

RICHARD [*staring at this unexpected turn*] I never thought of such a thing. [*Sardonic again*]. I see there is another side to domestic joy.

JUDITH [*angrily*] I would rather have a husband whom everybody respects than—than—

RICHARD. Than the devil's disciple. You are right; but I daresay your love helps him to be a good man, just as your hate helps me to be a bad one.

JUDITH. My husband has been very good to you. He has forgiven you for insulting him, and is trying to save you. Can you not forgive him for being so much better than you are? How dare you belittle him by putting yourself in his place?

RICHARD. Did I?

JUDITH. Yes, you did. You said that if anybody came in they would take us for man and—[*She stops, terrorstricken, as a squad of soldiers tramps past the window*]. The English soldiers! Oh, what do they—

RICHARD [*listening*] Sh!

A VOICE [*outside*] Halt! Four outside: two in with me.

Judith half rises, listening and looking with dilated eyes at Richard, who takes up his cup prosaically, and is drinking his tea when the latch goes up with a sharp click, and an English sergeant walks into the room with two privates, who post themselves at the door. He comes promptly to the table between them.

THE SERGEANT. Sorry to disturb you, mum. Duty! Anthony Anderson: I arrest you in King George's name as a rebel.

JUDITH [*pointing at Richard*] But that is not—[*He looks up quickly at her, with a face of iron. She stops her mouth hastily with the hand she has raised to indicate him, and stands staring affrightedly*].

THE SERGEANT. Come, parson: put your coat on and come along.

RICHARD. Yes: I'll come. [*He rises and takes a step towards his own coat; then recollects himself, and, with his back to the sergeant, moves his gaze slowly round the room without turning his head until he sees Anderson's black coat hanging up on the press. He goes composedly to it; takes it down; and puts it on. The idea of himself as a parson tickles him: he looks down at the black sleeve on his arm, and then smiles slyly at Judith, whose white face shews him that what she is painfully struggling to grasp is not the humor of the situation but its horror. He turns to the sergeant, who is approaching him with a pair of handcuffs hidden behind him, and says lightly*] Did you ever arrest a man of my cloth before, Sergeant?

THE SERGEANT [*instinctively respectful, half to the black coat, and half to Richard's good breeding*] Well, no sir. At least, only an army chaplain. [*Shewing the handcuffs*]. I'm sorry sir; but duty—

RICHARD. Just so, Sergeant. Well, I'm not ashamed of them: thank you kindly for the apology. [*He holds out his hands*].

SERGEANT [*not availing himself of the offer*] One gentleman to another, sir. Wouldnt you like to say a word to your missis, sir, before you go?

RICHARD [*smiling*] Oh, we shall meet again before—eh? [*meaning "before you hang me"*].

SERGEANT [*loudly, with ostentatious cheerfulness*] Oh, of course, of course. No call for the lady to distress herself. Still—[*in a lower voice, intended for Richard alone*] your last chance, sir.

They look at one another significantly for a moment. Then Richard exhales a deep breath and turns towards Judith.

RICHARD [*very distinctly*] My love. [*She looks at him, pitiably pale, and tries to answer, but cannot—tries also to come to him, but cannot trust herself to stand without the support of the table*]. This gallant gentleman is good enough to allow us a moment of leave-taking. [*The sergeant retires delicately and joins his men near the door*]. He is trying to spare you the truth; but you had better know it. Are you listening to me? [*She signifies assent*]. Do you understand that I am going to my death? [*She signifies that she understands*]. Remember, you must find our friend who was with us just now. Do you understand? [*She signifies yes*]. See that you get him safely out of harm's way. Dont for your life let him know of my danger; but if he finds it out, tell him that he cannot save me: they would hang him; and they would not spare me. And tell him that I am steadfast in my religion as he is in his, and that he may depend on me to the death. [*He turns to go, and meets the eyes of the sergeant, who looks a little suspicious. He considers a moment, and then, turning roguishly to Judith with something of a smile breaking through his earnestness, says*] And now, my dear, I am afraid the sergeant will not believe that you love me like a wife unless you give one kiss before I go.

He approaches her and holds out his arms. She quits the table and almost falls into them.

JUDITH [*the words choking her*] I ought to—it's murder—

RICHARD. No: only a kiss [*softly to her*] for his sake.

JUDITH. I cant. You must—

RICHARD [*folding her in his arms with an impulse of compassion for her distress*] My poor girl!

Judith, with a sudden effort, throws her arms round him; kisses him; and swoons away, dropping from his arms to the ground as if the kiss had killed her.

RICHARD [*going quickly to the sergeant*] Now, Sergeant: quick, before she comes to. The handcuffs. [*He puts out his hands*].

SERGEANT [*pocketing them*] Never mind, sir: I'll trust you. Youre a game one. You ought to a bin a soldier, sir. Between them two, please. [*The soldiers place themselves one before Richard and one behind him. The sergeant opens the door*].

RICHARD [*taking a last look round him*] Goodbye, wife: goodbye, home. Muffle the drums, and quick march!

The sergeant signs to the leading soldier to march. They file out quickly. * * * * * * * * * * * * * * * * * *When Anderson returns from*

Mrs Dudgeon's, he is astonished to find the room apparently empty and almost in darkness except for the glow from the fire; for one of the candles has burnt out, and the other is at its last flicker.

ANDERSON. Why, what on earth—? [*Calling*] Judith, Judith! [*He listens: there is no answer*]. Hm! [*He goes to the cupboard; takes a candle from the drawer; lights it at the flicker of the expiring one on the table; and looks wonderingly at the untasted meal by its light. Then he sticks it in the candlestick; takes off his hat; and scratches his head, much puzzled. This action causes him to look at the floor for the first time; and there he sees Judith lying motionless with her eyes closed. He runs to her and stoops beside her, lifting her head*]. Judith.

JUDITH [*waking; for her swoon has passed into the sleep of exhaustion after suffering*] Yes. Did you call? Whats the matter?

ANDERSON. Ive just come in and found you lying here with the candles burnt out and the tea poured out and cold. What has happened?

JUDITH [*still astray*] I dont know. Have I been asleep? I suppose — [*She stops blankly*], I dont know.

ANDERSON [*groaning*] Heaven forgive me, I left you alone with that scoundrel. [*Judith remembers. With an agonized cry, she clutches his shoulders and drags herself to her feet as he rises with her. He clasps her tenderly in his arms*]. My poor pet!

JUDITH [*frantically clinging to him*] What shall I do? Oh my God, what shall I do?

ANDERSON. Never mind, never mind, my dearest dear: it was my fault. Come: youre safe now; and youre not hurt, are you? [*He takes his arms from her to see whether she can stand*]. There: thats right, thats right. If only you are not hurt, nothing else matters.

JUDITH. No, no, no: I'm not hurt.

ANDERSON. Thank Heaven for that! Come now: [*leading her to the railed seat and making her sit down beside him*] sit down and rest: you can tell me about it tomorrow. Or [*misunderstanding her distress*] you shall not tell me at all if it worries you. There, there!

[*Cheerfully*] I'll make you some fresh tea: that will set you up again. [*He goes to the table, and empties the teapot into the slop bowl*].

JUDITH [*in a strained tone*] Tony.

ANDERSON. Yes, dear?

JUDITH. Do you think we are only in a dream now?

ANDERSON [*glancing round at her for a moment with a pang of anxiety, though he goes on steadily and cheerfully putting fresh tea into the pot*] Perhaps so, pet. But you may as well dream a cup of tea when youre about it.

JUDITH. Oh stop, stop. You dont know— [*Distracted, she buries her face in her knotted hands*].

ANDERSON [*breaking down and coming to her*] My dear, what is it? I cant bear it any longer: you must tell me. It was all my fault: I was mad to trust him.

JUDITH. No: dont say that. You mustnt say that. He—oh no, no: I cant. Tony: dont speak to me. Take my hands—both my hands. [*He takes them, wondering*]. Make me think of you, not of him. Theres danger, frightful danger; but it is your danger; and I cant keep thinking of it: I cant, I cant: my mind goes back to his danger. He must be saved—no: you must be saved: you, you, you. [*She springs up as if to do something or go somewhere, exclaiming*] Oh, Heaven help me?

ANDERSON [*keeping his seat and holding her hands with resolute composure*] Calmly, calmly, my pet. Youre quite distracted.

JUDITH. I may well be. I dont know what to do. I dont know what to do. [*Tearing her hands away*]. I must save him. [*Anderson rises in alarm as she runs wildly to the door. It is opened in her face by Essie, who hurries in full of anxiety. The surprise is so disagreeable to Judith that it brings her to her senses. Her tone is sharp and angry as she demands*] What do you want?

ESSIE. I was to come to you.

ANDERSON. Who told you to?

ESSIE [*staring at him, as if his presence astonished her*] Are you here?

JUDITH. Of course. Dont be foolish, child.

ANDERSON. Gently, dearest: youll frighten her. [*Going between them*]. Come here, Essie. [*She comes to him*]. Who sent you?

ESSIE. Dick. He sent me word by a soldier. I was to come here at once and do whatever Mrs Anderson told me.

ANDERSON [*enlightened*] A soldier! Ah, I see it all now! They have arrested Richard. [*Judith makes a gesture of despair*].

ESSIE. No. I asked the soldier. Dick's safe. But the soldier said you had been taken.

ANDERSON. I! [*Bewildered, he turns to Judith for an explanation*].

JUDITH [*coaxingly*] All right, dear: I understand. [*To Essie*] Thank you, Essie, for coming: but I dont need you now. You may go home.

ESSIE [*suspicious*] Are you sure Dick has not been touched? Perhaps he told the soldier to say it was the minister. [*Anxiously*] Mrs Anderson: do you think it can have been that?

ANDERSON. Tell her the truth if it is so, Judith. She will learn it from the first neighbor she meets in the street. [*Judith turns away and covers her eyes with her hands*].

ESSIE [*wailing*] But what will they do to him? Oh, what will they do to him? Will they hang him? [*Judith shudders convulsively, and throws herself into the chair in which Richard sat at the tea table*].

ANDERSON [*patting Essie's shoulder and trying to comfort her*] I hope not. I hope not. Perhaps if youre very quiet and patient, we may be able to help him in some way.

ESSIE. Yes—help him—yes, yes, yes. I'll be good.

ANDERSON. I must go to him at once, Judith.

JUDITH [*springing up*] Oh no. You must go away—far away, to some place of safety.

ANDERSON. Pooh!

JUDITH [*passionately*] Do you want to kill me? Do you think I can bear to live for days and days with every knock at the door—every footstep—giving me a spasm of terror? to lie awake for nights and nights in an agony of dread, listening for them to come and arrest you?

ANDERSON. Do you think it would be better to know that I had run away from my post at the first sign of danger?

JUDITH [*bitterly*] Oh, you wont go. I know it. Youll stay; and I shall go mad.

ANDERSON. My dear, your duty—

JUDITH [*fiercely*] What do I care about my duty?

ANDERSON [*shocked*] Judith!

JUDITH. I am doing my duty. I am clinging to my duty. My duty is to get you away, to save you, to leave him to his fate [*Essie utters a cry of distress and sinks on the chair at the fire, sobbing silently*]. My instinct is the same as hers—to save him above all things, though it would be so much better for him to die! so much greater! But I know you will take your own way as he took it. I have no power. [*She sits down sullenly on the railed seat*] I'm only a woman; I can do nothing but sit here and suffer. Only, tell him I tried to save you—that I did my best to save you.

ANDERSON. My dear, I am afraid he will be thinking more of his own danger than of mine.

JUDITH. Stop; or I shall hate you.

ANDERSON [*remonstrating*] Come, come, come! How am I to leave you if you talk like this? You are quite out of your senses. [*He turns to Essie*] Essie.

ESSIE [*eagerly rising and drying her eyes*] Yes?

ANDERSON. Just wait outside a moment, like a good girl; Mrs Anderson is not well. [*Essie looks doubtful*]. Never fear; I'll come to you presently; and I'll go to Dick.

ESSIE. You are sure you will go to him? [*Whispering*]. You wont let her prevent you?

ANDERSON [*smiling*] No, no; it's all right. All right. [*She goes*]. Thats a good girl. [*He closes the door, and returns to Judith*].

JUDITH [*seated—rigid*] You are going to your death.

ANDERSON [*quaintly*] Then I shall go in my best coat, dear. [*He turns to the press, beginning to take off his coat*]. Where—? [*He stares at the empty nail for a moment; then looks quickly round to the fire; strides across to it; and lifts Richard's coat*]. Why, my dear, it seems that he has gone in my best coat.

JUDITH [*still motionless*] Yes.

ANDERSON. Did the soldiers make a mistake?

JUDITH. Yes: they made a mistake.

ANDERSON. He might have told them. Poor fellow, he was too upset, I suppose.

JUDITH. Yes: he might have told them. So might I.

ANDERSON. Well, it's all very puzzling—almost funny. It's curious how these little things strike us even in the most—[*He breaks off and begins putting on Richard's coat*] I'd better take him his own coat. I know what he'll say—[*imitating Richard's sardonic manner*] "Anxious about my soul, Pastor, and also about your best coat." Eh?

JUDITH. Yes, that is just what he will say to you. [*Vacantly*] It doesnt matter: I shall never see either of you again.

ANDERSON [*rallying her*] Oh pooh, pooh, pooh! [*He sits down beside her*]. Is this how you keep your promise that I shant be ashamed of my brave wife?

JUDITH. No: this is how I break it. I cannot keep my promises to him: why should I keep my promises to you?

ANDERSON. Dont speak so strangely, my love. It sounds insincere to me. [*She looks unutterable reproach at him*].Yes, dear, nonsense is always insincere; and my dearest is talking nonsense. Just nonsense. [*Her face darkens into dumb obstinacy. She stares straight before her, and does not look at him again, absorbed in Richard's fate. He scans her face; sees that his rallying has produced no effect; and gives it up, making no further effort to conceal his anxiety*]. I wish I knew what has frightened you so. Was there a struggle? Did he fight?

JUDITH. No. He smiled.

ANDERSON. Did he realize his danger, do you think?

JUDITH. He realized yours.

ANDERSON. Mine!

JUDITH [*monotonously*] He said "See that you get him safely out of harm's way." I promised: I cant keep my promise. He said, "Dont for your life let him know of my danger." Ive told you of it. He said that if you found it out, you could not save him—that they will hang him and not spare you.

ANDERSON [*rising in generous indignation*] And you think that I will let a man with that much good in him die like a dog, when a few words might make him die like a Christian. I'm ashamed of you, Judith.

JUDITH. He will be steadfast in his religion as you are in yours; and you may depend on him to the death. He said so.

ANDERSON. God forgive him! What else did he say?

JUDITH. He said goodbye.

ANDERSON [*fidgeting nervously to and fro in great concern*] Poor fellow, poor fellow! You said goodbye to him in all kindness and charity, Judith, I hope.

JUDITH. I kissed him.

ANDERSON. What! Judith!

JUDITH. Are you angry?

ANDERSON. No, no. You were right: you were right. Poor fellow, poor fellow! [*Greatly distressed*] To be hanged like that at his age! And then did they take him away?

JUDITH [*wearily*] Then you were here: thats the next thing I remember. I suppose I fainted. Now bid me goodbye, Tony. Perhaps I shall faint again. I wish I could die.

ANDERSON. No, no, my dear: you must pull yourself together and be sensible. I am in no danger—not the least in the world.

JUDITH [*solemnly*] You are going to your death, Tony—your sure death, if God will let innocent men be murdered. They will not let you see him: they will arrest you the moment you give your name. It was for you the soldiers came.

ANDERSON [*thunderstruck*] For me!!! [*His fists clinch; his neck thickens; his face reddens; the fleshy purses under his eyes become injected with hot blood; the man of peace vanishes, transfigured into a choleric and formidable man of war. Still, she does not come out of her absorption to look at him: her eyes are steadfast with a mechanical reflection of Richard's steadfastness*].

JUDITH. He took your place: he is dying to save you. That is why he went in your coat. That is why I kissed him.

ANDERSON [*exploding*] Blood an' owns! [*His voice is rough and dominant, his gesture full of brute energy*]. Here! Essie, Essie!

ESSIE [*running in*] Yes.

ANDERSON [*impetuously*] Off with you as hard as you can run, to the inn. Tell them to saddle the fastest and strongest horse they have [*Judith rises breathless, and stares at him incredulously*]—the chestnut mare, if she's fresh—without a moment's delay. Go into the stable yard and tell the black man there that I'll give him a silver dollar if the horse is waiting for me when I come, and that I am close on your heels. Away with you. [*His energy sends Essie flying from the room. He pounces on his riding boots; rushes with them to the chair at the fire; and begins pulling them on*].

JUDITH [*unable to believe such a thing of him*] You are not going to him!

ANDERSON [*busy with the boots*] Going to him! What good would that do? [*Growling to himself as he gets the first boot on with a wrench*] I'll go to them, so I will. [*To Judith peremptorily*] Get me the pistols: I want them. And money, money: I want money—all the money in the house. [*He stoops over the other boot, grumbling*] A great satisfaction it would be to him to have my company on the gallows. [*He pulls on the boot*].

JUDITH. You are deserting him, then?

ANDERSON. Hold your tongue, woman; and get me the pistols. [*She goes to the press and takes from it a leather belt with two pistols, a powder horn, and a bag of bullets attached to it. She throws it on the table. Then she unlocks a drawer in the press and takes out a purse. Anderson grabs the belt and buckles it on, saying*] If they took him for me in my coat, perhaps theyll take me for him in his. [*Hitching the belt into its place*] Do I look like him?

JUDITH [*turning with the purse in her hand*] Horribly unlike him.

ANDERSON [*snatching the purse from her and emptying it on the table*] Hm! We shall see.

JUDITH [*sitting down helplessly*] Is it of any use to pray, do you think, Tony?

ANDERSON [*counting the money*] Pray! Can we pray Swindon's rope off Richard's neck?

JUDITH. God may soften Major Swindon's heart.

ANDERSON [*contemptuously—pocketing a handful of money*] Let him, then. I am not God; and I must go to work another way. [*Judith gasps at the blasphemy. He throws the purse on the table*]. Keep that. Ive taken 25 dollars.

JUDITH. Have you forgotten even that you are a minister?

ANDERSON. Minister be—faugh! My hat: wheres my hat? [*He snatches up hat and cloak, and puts both on in hot haste*] Now listen, you. If you can get a word with him by pretending youre his wife, tell him to hold his tongue until morning: that will give me all the start I need.

JUDITH [*solemnly*] You may depend on him to the death.

ANDERSON. Youre a fool, a fool, Judith. [*For a moment checking the torrent of his haste, and speaking with something of his old quiet and impressive conviction*] You dont know the man youre married to. [*Essie returns. He swoops at her at once*]. Well: is the horse ready?

ESSIE [*breathless*] It will be ready when you come.

ANDERSON. Good. [*He makes for the door*].

JUDITH [*rising and stretching out her arms after him involuntarily*] Wont you say goodbye?

ANDERSON. And waste another half minute! Psha! [*He rushes out like an avalanche*].

ESSIE [*hurrying to Judith*] He has gone to save Richard, hasnt he?

JUDITH. To save Richard! No: Richard has saved him. He has gone to save himself. Richard must die.

Essie screams with terror and falls on her knees, hiding her face. Judith, without heeding her, looks rigidly straight in front of her, at the vision of Richard, dying.

ACT III

Early next morning the sergeant, at the British headquarters in the Town Hall, unlocks the door of a little empty panelled waiting room, and invites Judith to enter. She has had a bad night, probably a rather delirious one; for even in the reality of the raw morning, her fixed gaze comes back at moments when her attention is not strongly held.

The sergeant considers that her feelings do her credit, and is sympathetic in an encouraging military way. Being a fine figure of a man, vain of his uniform and of his rank, he feels specially qualified, in a respectful way, to console her.

SERGEANT. You can have a quiet word with him here, mum.

JUDITH. Shall I have long to wait?

SERGEANT. No, mum, not a minute. We kep him in the Bridewell for the night; and he's just been brought over here for the court martial. Dont fret, mum: he slep like a child, and has made a rare good breakfast.

JUDITH [*incredulously*] He is in good spirits!

SERGEANT. Tip top, mum. The chaplain looked in to see him last night; and he won seventeen shillings off him at spoil five. He spent it among us like the gentleman he is. Duty's duty, mum, of course; but youre among friends here. [*The tramp of a couple of soldiers is heard approaching*]. There: I think he's coming. [*Richard comes in, without a sign of care or captivity in his bearing. The sergeant nods to the two soldiers, and shows them the key of the room in his hand. They withdraw*]. Your good lady, sir.

RICHARD [*going to her*] What! My wife. My adored one. [*He takes her hand and kisses it with a perverse, raffish gallantry*]. How long do you allow a brokenhearted husband for leave-taking, Sergeant?

SERGEANT. As long as we can, sir. We shall not disturb you till the court sits.

RICHARD. But it has struck the hour.

SERGEANT. So it has, sir; but theres a delay. General Burgoyne's just arrived—Gentlemanly Johnny we call him, sir—and he wont have done finding fault with everything this side of half past. I know him, sir: I served with him in Portugal. You may count on twenty minutes, sir; and by your leave I wont waste any more of them. [*He goes out, locking the door. Richard immediately drops his raffish manner and turns to Judith with considerate sincerity*].

RICHARD. Mrs Anderson: this visit is very kind of you. And how are you after last night? I had to leave you before you recovered; but I sent word to Essie to go and look after you. Did she understand the message?

JUDITH [*breathless and urgent*] Oh, dont think of me: I havnt come here to talk about myself. Are they going to—to—[*meaning "to hang you"*]?

RICHARD [*whimsically*] At noon, punctually. At least, that was when they disposed of Uncle Peter. [*She shudders*]. Is your husband safe? Is he on the wing?

JUDITH. He is no longer my husband.

RICHARD [*opening his eyes wide*] Eh?

JUDITH. I disobeyed you. I told him everything. I expected him to come here and save you. I wanted him to come here and save you. He ran away instead.

RICHARD. Well, thats what I meant him to do. What good would his staying have done? Theyd only have hanged us both.

JUDITH [*with reproachful earnestness*] Richard Dudgeon: on your honor, what would you have done in his place?

RICHARD. Exactly what he has done, of course.

JUDITH. Oh, why will you not be simple with me—honest and straightforward? If you are so selfish as that, why did you let them take you last night?

RICHARD [*gaily*] Upon my life, Mrs Anderson, I dont know. Ive been asking myself that question ever since; and I can find no manner of reason for acting as I did.

JUDITH. You know you did it for his sake, believing he was a more worthy man than yourself.

RICHARD [*laughing*] Oho! No: thats a very pretty reason, I must say; but I'm not so modest as that. No: it wasnt for his sake.

JUDITH [*after a pause, during which she looks shamefacedly at him, blushing painfully*] Was it for my sake?

RICHARD [*gallantly*] Well, you had a hand in it. It must have been a little for your sake. You let them take me, at all events.

JUDITH. Oh, do you think I have not been telling myself that all night? Your death will be at my door. [*Impulsively, she gives him her hand, and adds, with intense earnestness*] If I could save you as you saved him, I would do it, no matter how cruel the death was.

RICHARD [*holding her hand and smiling, but keeping her almost at arms length*] I am very sure I shouldnt let you.

JUDITH. Dont you see that I can save you?

RICHARD. How? by changing clothes with me, eh?

JUDITH [*disengaging her hand to touch his lips with it*] Dont [*meaning "Dont jest"*]. No: by telling the court who you really are.

RICHARD [*frowning*] No use: they wouldnt spare me; and it would spoil half his chance of escaping. They are determined to cow us by making an example of somebody on that gallows to-day. Well, let us cow them by showing that we can stand by one another to the death. That is the only force that can send Burgoyne back across the Atlantic and make America a nation.

JUDITH [*impatiently*] Oh, what does all that matter?

RICHARD [*laughing*] True: what does it matter? what does anything matter? You see, men have these strange notions, Mrs Anderson; and women see the folly of them.

JUDITH. Women have to lose those they love through them.

RICHARD. They can easily get fresh lovers.

JUDITH [*revolted*] Oh! [*Vehemently*] Do you realize that you are going to kill yourself?

RICHARD. The only man I have any right to kill, Mrs Anderson. Dont be concerned: no woman will lose her lover through my death. [*Smiling*] Bless you, nobody cares for me. Have you heard that my mother is dead?

70

JUDITH. Dead!

RICHARD. Of heart disease—in the night. Her last word to me was her curse: I dont think I could have borne her blessing. My other relatives will not grieve much on my account. Essie will cry for a day or two; but I have provided for her: I made my own will last night.

JUDITH [*stonily, after a moment's silence*] And I!

RICHARD [*surprised*] You?

JUDITH. Yes, I. Am I not to care at all?

RICHARD [*gaily and bluntly*] Not a scrap. Oh, you expressed your feelings towards me very frankly yesterday. What happened may have softened you for the moment; but believe me, Mrs Anderson, you dont like a bone in my skin or a hair on my head. I shall be as good a riddance at 12 today as I should have been at 12 yesterday.

JUDITH [*her voice trembling*] What can I do to shew you that you are mistaken.

RICHARD. Dont trouble. I'll give you credit for liking me a little better than you did. All I say is that my death will not break your heart.

JUDITH [*almost in a whisper*] How do you know? [*She puts her hands on his shoulders and looks intently at him*].

RICHARD [*amazed—divining the truth*] Mrs Anderson! [*The bell of the town clock strikes the quarter. He collects himself, and removes her hands, saying rather coldly*] Excuse me: they will be here for me presently. It is too late.

JUDITH. It is not too late. Call me as witness: they will never kill you when they know how heroically you have acted.

RICHARD [*with some scorn*] Indeed! But if I dont go through with it, where will the heroism be? I shall simply have tricked them; and theyll hang me for that like a dog. Serve me right too!

JUDITH [*wildly*] Oh, I believe you want to die.

RICHARD [*obstinately*] No I dont.

JUDITH. Then why not try to save yourself? I implore you— listen. You said just now that you saved him for my sake—yes

71

[*clutching him as he recoils with a gesture of denial*] a little for my sake. Well, save yourself for my sake. And I will go with you to the end of the world.

RICHARD [*taking her by the wrists and holding her a little way from him, looking steadily at her*] Judith.

JUDITH [*breathless—delighted at the name*] Yes.

RICHARD. If I said—to please you—that I did what I did ever so little for your sake, I lied as men always lie to women. You know how much I have lived with worthless men—aye, and worthless women too. Well, they could all rise to some sort of goodness and kindness when they were in love [*the word love comes from him with true Puritan scorn*]. That has taught me to set very little store by the goodness that only comes out red hot. What I did last night, I did in cold blood, caring not half so much for your husband, or [*ruthlessly*] for you [*she droops, stricken*] as I do for myself. I had no motive and no interest: all I can tell you is that when it came to the point whether I would take my neck out of the noose and put another man's into it, I would not do it. I dont know why not: I see myself as a fool for my pains; but I could not and I cannot. I have been brought up standing by the law of my own nature; and I may not go against it, gallows or no gallows. [*She has slowly raised her head and is now looking full at him*]. I should have done the same for any other man in the town, or any other man's wife. [*Releasing her*] Do you understand that?

JUDITH. Yes: you mean that you do not love me.

RICHARD [*revolted—with fierce contempt*] Is that all it means to you?

JUDITH. What more—what worse—can it mean to me? [*The sergeant knocks. The blow on the door jars on her heart*]. Oh, one moment more. [*She throws herself on her knees*]. I pray to you—

RICHARD. Hush! [*Calling*] Come in. [*The sergeant unlocks the door and opens it. The guard is with him*].

SERGEANT [*coming in*] Time's up, sir.

RICHARD. Quite ready, Sergeant. Now, my dear. [*He attempts to raise her*].

JUDITH [*clinging to him*] Only one thing more—I entreat, I implore you. Let me be present in the court. I have seen Major Swindon: he said I should be allowed if you asked it. You will ask it. It is my last request: I shall never ask you anything again. [*She clasps his knee*]. I beg and pray it of you.

RICHARD. If I do, will you be silent?

JUDITH. Yes.

RICHARD. You will keep faith?

JUDITH. I will keep—[*She breaks down, sobbing*].

RICHARD [*taking her arm to lift her*] Just—her other arm, Sergeant.

They go out, she sobbing convulsively, supported by the two men.

Meanwhile, the Council Chamber is ready for the court martial. It is a large, lofty room, with a chair of state in the middle under a tall canopy with a gilt crown, and maroon curtains with the royal monogram G.R. In front of the chair is a table, also draped in maroon, with a bell, a heavy inkstand, and writing materials on it. Several chairs are set at the table. The door is at the right hand of the occupant of the chair of state when it has an occupant: at present it is empty. Major Swindon, a pale, sandy-haired, very conscientious looking man of about 45, sits at the end of the table with his back to the door, writing. He is alone until the sergeant announces the General in a subdued manner which suggests that Gentlemanly Johnny has been making his presence felt rather heavily.

SERGEANT. The General, sir.

Swindon rises hastily. The general comes in: the sergeant goes out. General Burgoyne is 55, and very well preserved. He is a man of fashion, gallant enough to have made a distinguished marriage by an elopement, witty enough to write successful comedies, aristocratically-connected enough to have had opportunities of high military distinction. His eyes, large, brilliant, apprehensive, and intelligent, are his most remarkable feature: without them his fine nose and small mouth would suggest rather more fastidiousness and less force than go to the making of a first rate general. Just now the eyes are angry and tragic, and the mouth and the nostrils tense.

BURGOYNE. Major Swindon, I presume.

SWINDON. Yes. General Burgoyne, if I mistake not. [*They bow to one another ceremoniously*]. I am glad to have the support of your presence this morning. It is not particularly lively business, hanging this poor devil of a minister.

BURGOYNE [*throwing himself into Swindon's chair*] No, sir, it is not. It is making too much of the fellow to execute him: what more could you have done if he had been a member of the Church of England? Martyrdom, sir, is what these people like: it is the only way in which a man can become famous without ability. However, you have committed us to hanging him; and the sooner he is hanged the better.

SWINDON. We have arranged it for 12 o'clock. Nothing remains to be done except to try him.

BURGOYNE [*looking at him with suppressed anger*] Nothing—except to save your own necks, perhaps. Have you heard the news from Springtown?

SWINDON. Nothing special. The latest reports are satisfactory.

BURGOYNE [*rising in amazement*] Satisfactory, sir! Satisfactory!! [*He stares at him for a moment, and then adds, with grim intensity*] I am glad you take that view of them.

SWINDON [*puzzled*] Do I understand that in your opinion—

BURGOYNE. I do not express my opinion. I never stoop to that habit of profane language which unfortunately coarsens our profession. If I did, sir, perhaps I should be able to express my opinion of the news from Springtown—the news which you [*severely*] have apparently not heard. How soon do you get news from your supports here?—in the course of a month, eh?

SWINDON [*turning sulky*] I suppose the reports have been taken to you, sir, instead of to me. Is there anything serious?

BURGOYNE [*taking a report from his pocket and holding it up*] Springtown's in the hands of the rebels. [*He throws the report on the table*].

SWINDON [*aghast*] Since yesterday!

BURGOYNE. Since two o'clock this morning. Perhaps we shall

be in their hands before two o'clock tomorrow morning. Have you thought of that?

SWINDON [*confidently*] As to that, General, the British soldier will give a good account of himself.

BURGOYNE [*bitterly*] And therefore, I suppose, sir, the British officer need not know his business: the British soldier will get him out of all his blunders with the bayonet. In future, sir, I must ask you to be a little less generous with the blood of your men, and a little more generous with your own brains.

SWINDON. I am sorry I cannot pretend to your intellectual eminence, sir. I can only do my best, and rely on the devotion of my countrymen.

BURGOYNE [*suddenly becoming suavely sarcastic*] May I ask are you writing a melodrama, Major Swindon?

SWINDON [*flushing*] No, sir.

BURGOYNE. What a pity! What a pity! [*Dropping his sarcastic tone and facing him suddenly and seriously*] Do you at all realize, sir, that we háve nothing standing between us and destruction but our own bluff and the sheepishness of these colonists? They are men of the same English stock as ourselves: six to one of us [*repeating it emphatically*] six to one, sir; and nearly half our troops are Hessians, Brunswickers, German dragoons, and Indians with scalping knives. These are the countrymen on whose devotion you rely! Suppose the colonists find a leader! Suppose the news from Springtown should turn out to mean that they have already found a leader! What shall we do then? Eh?

SWINDON [*sullenly*] Our duty, sir, I presume.

BURGOYNE [*again sarcastic—giving him up as a fool*] Quite so, quite so. Thank you, Major Swindon, thank you. Now youve settled the question, sir—thrown a flood of light on the situation. What a comfort to me to feel that I have at my side so devoted and able an officer to support me in this emergency! I think, sir, it will probably relieve both our feelings if we proceed to hang this dissenter without further delay [*he strikes the bell*] especially as I am debarred by my principles from the customary military vent for my feelings. [*The sergeant appears*]. Bring your man in.

SERGEANT. Yes, sir.

BURGOYNE. And mention to any officer you may meet that the court cannot wait any longer for him.

SWINDON [*keeping his temper with difficulty*] The staff is perfectly ready, sir. They have been waiting your convenience for fully half an hour. Perfectly ready, sir.

BURGOYNE [*blandly*] So am I. [*Several officers come in and take their seats. One of them sits at the end of the table farthest from the door, and acts throughout as clerk of the court, making notes of the proceedings. The uniforms are those of the 9th, 20th, 21st, 24th, 47th, 53rd, and 62nd British Infantry. One officer is a Major General of the Royal Artillery. There are also German officers of the Hessian Rifles, and of German dragoon and Brunswicker regiments*]. Oh, good morning, gentlemen. Sorry to disturb you, I am sure. Very good of you to spare us a few moments.

SWINDON. Will you preside, sir?

BURGOYNE [*becoming additionally polished, lofty, sarcastic, and urbane now that he is in public*] No, sir: I feel my own deficiencies too keenly to presume so far. If you will kindly allow me, I will sit at the feet of Gamaliel. [*He takes the chair at the end of the table next the door, and motions Swindon to the chair of state, waiting for him to be seated before sitting down himself*].

SWINDON [*greatly annoyed*] As you please, sir. I am only trying to do my duty under excessively trying circumstances. [*He takes his place in the chair of state*].

Burgoyne, relaxing his studied demeanor for the moment, sits down and begins to read the report with knitted brows and careworn looks, reflecting on his desperate situation and Swindon's uselessness. Richard is brought in. Judith walks beside him. Two soldiers precede and two follow him, with the sergeant in command. They cross the room to the wall opposite the door; but when Richard has just passed before the chair of state the sergeant stops him with a touch on the arm, and posts himself behind him, at his elbow. Judith stands timidly at the wall. The four soldiers place themselves in a squad near her.

BURGOYNE [*looking up and seeing Judith*] Who is that woman?

SERGEANT. Prisoner's wife, sir.

SWINDON [*nervously*] She begged me to allow her to be present; and I thought—

BURGOYNE [*completing the sentence for him ironically*] You thought it would be a pleasure for her. Quite so, quite so. [*Blandly*] Give the lady a chair; and make her thoroughly comfortable.

The sergeant fetches a chair and places it near Richard.

JUDITH. Thank you, sir. [*She sits down after an awestricken curtsy to Burgoyne, which he acknowledges by a dignified bend of his head*].

SWINDON [*to Richard, sharply*] Your name, sir?

RICHARD [*affable, but obstinate*] Come: you dont mean to say that youve brought me here without knowing who I am?

SWINDON. As a matter of form, sir, give your name.

RICHARD. As a matter of form then, my name is Anthony Anderson, Presbyterian minister in this town.

BURGOYNE [*interested*] Indeed! Pray, Mr Anderson, what do you gentlemen believe?

RICHARD. I shall be happy to explain if time is allowed me. I cannot undertake to complete your conversion in less than a fortnight.

SWINDON [*snubbing him*] We are not here to discuss your views.

BURGOYNE [*with an elaborate bow to the unfortunate Swindon*] I stand rebuked.

SWINDON [*embarrassed*] Oh, not you, I as—

BURGOYNE. Dont mention it. [*To Richard, very politely*] Any political views, Mr Anderson?

RICHARD. I understand that that is just what we are here to find out.

SWINDON [*severely*] Do you mean to deny that you are a rebel?

RICHARD. I am an American, sir.

SWINDON. What do you expect me to think of that speech, Mr Anderson?

RICHARD. I never expect a soldier to think, sir.

77

Burgoyne is boundlessly delighted by this retort, which almost reconciles him to the loss of America.

SWINDON [*whitening with anger*] I advise you not to be insolent, prisoner.

RICHARD. You cant help yourself, General. When you make up your mind to hang a man, you put yourself at a disadvantage with him. Why should I be civil to you? I may as well be hanged for a sheep as a lamb.

SWINDON. You have no right to assume that the court has made up its mind without a fair trial. And you will please not address me as General. I am Major Swindon.

RICHARD. A thousand pardons. I thought I had the honor of addressing Gentlemanly Johnny.

Sensation among the officers. The sergeant has a narrow escape from a guffaw.

BURGOYNE [*with extreme suavity*] I believe I am Gentlemanly Johnny, sir, at your service. My more intimate friends call me General Burgoyne. [*Richard bows with perfect politeness*]. You will understand, sir, I hope, since you seem to be a gentleman and a man of some spirit in spite of your calling, that if we should have the misfortune to hang you, we shall do so as a mere matter of political necessity and military duty, without any personal ill-feeling.

RICHARD. Oh, quite so. That makes all the difference in the world, of course.

They all smile in spite of themselves; and some of the younger officers burst out laughing.

JUDITH [*her dread and horror deepening at every one of these jests and compliments*] How can you?

RICHARD. You promised to be silent.

BURGOYNE [*to Judith, with studied courtesy*] Believe me, Madam, your husband is placing us under the greatest obligation by taking this very disagreeable business so thoroughly in the spirit of a gentleman. Sergeant: give Mr Anderson a chair. [*The sergeant does so. Richard sits down*]. Now, Major Swindon: we are waiting for you.

SWINDON. You are aware, I presume, Mr Anderson, of your obligations as a subject of His Majesty King George the Third.

RICHARD. I am aware, sir, that His Majesty King George the Third is about to hang me because I object to Lord North's robbing me.

SWINDON. That is a treasonable speech, sir.

RICHARD [*briefly*] Yes. I meant it to be.

BURGOYNE [*strongly deprecating this line of defence, but still polite*] Dont you think, Mr Anderson, that this is rather—if you will excuse the word—a vulgar line to take? Why should you cry out robbery because of a stamp duty and a tea duty and so forth? After all, it is the essence of your position as a gentleman that you pay with a good grace.

RICHARD. It is not the money, General. But to be swindled by a pig-headed lunatic like King George—

SWINDON [*scandalized*] Chut, sir—silence!

SERGEANT [*in stentorian tones, greatly shocked*] Silence!

BURGOYNE [*unruffled*] Ah, this is another point of view. My position does not allow of my going into that, except in private. But [*shrugging his shoulders*] of course, Mr Anderson, if you are determined to be hanged [*Judith flinches*] there's nothing more to be said. An unusual taste! however [*with a final shrug*]—!

SWINDON [*To Burgoyne*] Shall we call witnesses?

RICHARD. What need is there of witnesses? If the townspeople here had listened to me, you would have found the streets barricaded, the houses loopholed, and the people in arms to hold the town against you to the last man. But you arrived, unfortunately, before we had got out of the talking stage; and then it was too late.

SWINDON [*severely*] Well, sir, we shall teach you and your townspeople a lesson they will not forget. Have you anything more to say?

RICHARD. I think you might have the decency to treat me as a prisoner of war, and shoot me like a man instead of hanging me like a dog.

BURGOYNE [*sympathetically*] Now there, Mr Anderson, you

talk like a civilian, if you will excuse my saying so. Have you any idea of the average marksmanship of the army of His Majesty King George the Third? If we make you up a firing party, what will happen? Half of them will miss you: the rest will make a mess of the business and leave you to the provo-marshal's pistol. Whereas we can hang you in a perfectly workmanlike and agreeable way. [*Kindly*] Let me persuade you to be hanged, Mr Anderson?

JUDITH [*sick with horror*] My God!

RICHARD [*To Judith*] Your promise! [*To Burgoyne*] Thank you, General: that view of the case did not occur to me before. To oblige you, I withdraw my objection to the rope. Hang me, by all means.

BURGOYNE [*smoothly*] Will 12 o'clock suit you, Mr Anderson?

RICHARD. I shall be at your disposal then, General.

BURGOYNE [*rising*] Nothing more to be said, gentlemen. [*They all rise*].

JUDITH [*rushing to the table*] Oh, you are not going to murder a man like that, without a proper trial—without thinking of what you are doing—without—[*she cannot find words*].

RICHARD. Is this how you keep your promise?

JUDITH. If I am not to speak, you must. Defend yourself: save yourself: tell them the truth.

RICHARD [*worriedly*] I have told them truth enough to hang me ten times over. If you say another word you will risk other lives; but you will not save mine.

BURGOYNE. My good lady, our only desire is to save unpleasantness. What satisfaction would it give you to have a solemn fuss made, with my friend Swindon in a black cap and so forth? I am sure we are greatly indebted to the admirable tact and gentlemanly feeling shewn by your husband.

JUDITH [*throwing the words in his face*] Oh, you are mad. Is it nothing to you what wicked thing you do if only you do it like a gentleman? Is it nothing to you whether you are a murderer or not, if only you murder in a red coat? [*Desperately*] You shall not hang him: that man is not my husband.

The officers look at one another, and whisper: some of the Germans asking their neighbors to explain what the woman had said. Burgoyne, who has been visibly shaken by Judith's reproach, recovers himself promptly at this new development. Richard meanwhile raises his voice above the buzz.

RICHARD. I appeal to you, gentlemen, to put an end to this. She will not believe that she cannot save me. Break up the court.

BURGOYNE [*in a voice so quiet and firm that it restores silence at once*] One moment, Mr Anderson. One moment, gentlemen. [*He resumes his seat. Swindon and the officers follow his example*]. Let me understand you clearly, madam. Do you mean that this gentleman is not your husband, or merely—I wish to put this with all delicacy—that you are not his wife?

JUDITH. I dont know what you mean. I say that he is not my husband—that my husband has escaped. This man took his place to save him. Ask anyone in the town—send out into the street for the first person you find there, and bring him in as a witness. He will tell you that the prisoner is not Anthony Anderson.

BURGOYNE [*quietly, as before*] Sergeant.

SERGEANT. Yes, sir.

BURGOYNE. Go out into the street and bring in the first townsman you see there.

SERGEANT [*making for the door*] Yes, sir.

BURGOYNE [*as the sergeant passes*] The first clean, sober townsman you see.

SERGEANT. Yes, sir. [*He goes out*].

BURGOYNE. Sit down, Mr Anderson—if I may call you so for the present. [*Richard sits down*]. Sit down, madam, whilst we wait. Give the lady a newspaper.

RICHARD [*indignantly*] Shame!

BURGOYNE [*keenly, with a half smile*] If you are not her husband, sir, the case is not a serious one—for her [*Richard bites his lip, silenced*].

JUDITH [*to Richard, as she returns to her seat*] I couldnt help it. [*He shakes his head. She sits down*].

BURGOYNE. You will understand of course, Mr Anderson, that you must not build on this little incident. We are bound to make an example of somebody.

RICHARD. I quite understand. I suppose theres no use in my explaining.

BURGOYNE. I think we should prefer independent testimony, if you dont mind.

The sergeant, with a packet of papers in his hand, returns conducting Christy, who is much scared.

SERGEANT [*giving Burgoyne the packet*] Dispatches, sir. Delivered by a corporal of the 33rd. Dead beat with hard riding, sir.

Burgoyne opens the dispatches, and presently becomes absorbed in them. They are so serious as to take his attention completely from the court martial.

THE SERGEANT [*to Christy*] Now then. Attention; and take your hat off. [*He posts himself in charge of Christy, who stands on Burgoyne's side of the court*].

RICHARD [*in his usual bullying tone to Christy*] Dont be frightened, you fool: youre only wanted as a witness. Theyre not going to hang you.

SWINDON. Whats your name?

CHRISTY. Christy.

RICHARD [*impatiently*] Christopher Dudgeon, you blatant idiot. Give your full name.

SWINDON. Be silent, prisoner. You must not prompt the witness.

RICHARD. Very well. But I warn you youll get nothing out of him unless you shake it out of him. He has been too well brought up by a pious mother to have any sense or manhood left in him.

BURGOYNE [*springing up and speaking to the sergeant in a startling voice*] Where is the man who brought these?

SERGEANT. In the guard-room, sir.

Burgoyne goes out with a haste that sets the officers exchanging looks.

SWINDON [*to Christy*] Do you know Anthony Anderson, the Presbyterian minister?

CHRISTY. Of course I do [*implying that Swindon must be an ass not to know it*].

SWINDON. Is he here?

CHRISTY [*staring round*] I dont know.

SWINDON. Do you see him?

CHRISTY. No.

SWINDON. You seem to know the prisoner?

CHRISTY. Do you mean Dick?

SWINDON. Which is Dick?

CHRISTY [*pointing to Richard*] Him.

SWINDON. What is his name?

CHRISTY. Dick.

RICHARD. Answer properly, you jumping jackass. What do they know about Dick?

CHRISTY. Well, you are Dick, aint you? What am I to say?

SWINDON. Address me, sir; and do you, prisoner, be silent. Tell us who the prisoner is.

CHRISTY. He's my brother Dick—Richard—Richard Dudgeon.

SWINDON. Your brother!

CHRISTY. Yes.

SWINDON. You are sure he is not Anderson.

CHRISTY. Who?

RICHARD [*exasperatedly*] Me, me, me, you—

SWINDON. Silence, sir.

SERGEANT [*shouting*] Silence.

RICHARD [*impatiently*] Yah! [*To Christy*] He wants to know am I Minister Anderson. Tell him, and stop grinning like a zany.

CHRISTY [*grinning more than ever*] You Pastor Anderson! [*To Swindon*] Why, Mr Anderson's a minister—a very good man; and Dick's a bad character: the respectable people wont speak to him. He's the bad brother: I'm the good one. [*The officers laugh outright. The soldiers grin*].

SWINDON. Who arrested this man?

83

SERGEANT. I did, sir. I found him in the minister's house, sitting at tea with the lady with his coat off, quite at home. If he isnt married to her, he ought to be.

SWINDON. Did he answer to the minister's name?

SERGEANT. Yes, sir, but not to a minister's nature. You ask the chaplain, sir.

SWINDON [*to Richard, threateningly*] So, sir, you have attempted to cheat us. And your name is Richard Dudgeon?

RICHARD. Youve found it out at last, have you?

SWINDON. Dudgeon is a name well known to us, eh?

RICHARD. Yes: Peter Dudgeon, whom you murdered, was my uncle.

SWINDON. Hm! [*He compresses his lips, and looks at Richard with vindictive gravity*].

CHRISTY. Are they going to hang you, Dick?

RICHARD. Yes. Get out: theyve done with you.

CHRISTY. And I may keep the china peacocks?

RICHARD [*jumping up*] Get out. G e t out, you blithering baboon, you. [*Christy flies, panicstricken*].

SWINDON [*rising—all rise*] Since you have taken the minister's place, Richard Dudgeon, you shall go through with it. The execution will take place at 12 o'clock as arranged; and unless Anderson surrenders before then, you shall take his place on the gallows. Sergeant: take your man out.

JUDITH [*distracted*] No, no—

SWINDON [*fiercely, dreading a renewal of her entreaties*] Take that woman away.

RICHARD [*springing across the table with a tiger-like bound, and seizing Swindon by the throat*] You infernal scoundrel—

The sergeant rushes to the rescue from one side, the soldiers from the other. They seize Richard and drag him back to his place. Swindon, who has been thrown supine on the table, rises, arranging his stock. He is about to speak, when he is anticipated by Burgoyne, who has just appeared at the door with two papers in his hand: a white letter and a blue dispatch.

BURGOYNE [*advancing to the table, elaborately cool*] What is this? Whats happening? Mr Anderson: I'm astonished at you.

RICHARD. I am sorry I disturbed you, General. I merely wanted to strangle your understrapper there. [*Breaking out violently at Swindon*] Why do you raise the devil in me by bullying the woman like that? You oatmeal faced dog, I'd twist your cursed head off with the greatest satisfaction. [*He puts out his hands to the sergeant*] Here: handcuff me, will you; or I'll not undertake to keep my fingers off him.

The sergeant takes out a pair of handcuffs and looks to Burgoyne for instructions.

BURGOYNE. Have you addressed profane language to the lady, Major Swindon?

SWINDON [*very angry*] No, sir, certainly not. That question should not have been put to me. I ordered the woman to be removed, as she was disorderly; and the fellow sprang at me. Put away those handcuffs. I am perfectly able to take care of myself.

RICHARD. Now you talk like a man, I have no quarrel with you.

BURGOYNE. Mr Anderson—

SWINDON. His name is Dudgeon, sir, Richard Dudgeon. He is an impostor.

BURGOYNE [*brusquely*] Nonsense, sir: you hanged Dudgeon at Springtown.

RICHARD. It was my uncle, General.

BURGOYNE. Oh, your uncle. [*To Swindon, handsomely*] I beg your pardon, Major Swindon. [*Swindon acknowledges the apology stiffly. Burgoyne turns to Richard*]. We are somewhat unfortunate in our relations with your family. Well, Mr Dudgeon, what I wanted to ask you is this. Who is [*reading the name from the letter*] William Maindeck Parshotter?

RICHARD. He is the Mayor of Springtown.

BURGOYNE. Is William—Maindeck and so on—a man of his word?

RICHARD. Is he selling you anything?

BURGOYNE. No.

RICHARD. Then you may depend on him.

BURGOYNE. Thank you, Mr—'m Dudgeon. By the way, since you are not Mr Anderson, do we still—eh, Major Swindon? [*meaning "do we still hang him?"*]

RICHARD. The arrangements are unaltered, General.

BURGOYNE. Ah, indeed. I am sorry. Good morning, Mr Dudgeon. Good morning, madam.

RICHARD [*interrupting Judith almost fiercely as she is about to make some wild appeal, and taking her arm resolutely*] Not one word more. Come.

She looks imploringly at him, but is overborne by his determination. They are marched out by the four soldiers: the sergeant very sulky, walking between Swindon and Richard, whom he watches as if he were a dangerous animal.

BURGOYNE. Gentlemen: we need not detain you. Major Swindon: a word with you. [*The officers go out. Burgoyne waits with unruffled serenity until the last of them disappears. Then he becomes very grave, and addresses Swindon for the first time without his title*]. Swindon: do you know what this is [*shewing him the letter*]?

SWINDON. What?

BURGOYNE. A demand for a safe-conduct for an officer of their militia to come here and arrange terms with us.

SWINDON. Oh, they are giving in.

BURGOYNE. They add that they are sending the man who raised Springtown last night and drove us out; so that we may know that we are dealing with an officer of importance.

SWINDON. Pooh!

BURGOYNE. He will be fully empowered to arrange the terms of —guess what.

SWINDON. Their surrender, I hope.

BURGOYNE. No: our evacuation of the town. They offer us just six hours to clear out.

SWINDON. What monstrous impudence!

BURGOYNE. What shall we do, eh?

SWINDON. March on Springtown and strike a decisive blow at once.

BURGOYNE [*quietly*] Hm! [*Turning to the door*] Come to the adjutant's office.

SWINDON. What for?

BURGOYNE. To write out that safe-conduct. [*He puts his hand to the door knob to open it*].

SWINDON [*who has not budged*] General Burgoyne.

BURGOYNE [*returning*] Sir?

SWINDON. It is my duty to tell you, sir, that I do not consider the threats of a mob of rebellious tradesmen a sufficient reason for our giving way.

BURGOYNE [*imperturbable*] Suppose I resign my command to you, what will you do?

SWINDON. I will undertake to do what we have marched south from Quebec to do, and what General Howe has marched north from New York to do: effect a junction at Albany and wipe out the rebel army with our united forces.

BURGOYNE [*enigmatically*] And will you wipe out our enemies in London, too?

SWINDON. In London! What enemies?

BURGOYNE [*forcibly*] Jobbery and snobbery, incompetence and Red Tape. [*He holds up the dispatch and adds, with despair in his face and voice*] I have just learnt, sir, that General Howe is still in New York.

SWINDON [*thunderstruck*] Good God! He has disobeyed orders!

BURGOYNE [*with sardonic calm*] He has received no orders, sir. Some gentleman in London forgot to dispatch them: he was leaving town for his holiday, I believe. To avoid upsetting his arrangements, England will lose her American colonies; and in a few days you and I will be at Saratoga with 5,000 men to face 18,000 rebels in an impregnable position.

SWINDON [*appalled*] Impossible?

BURGOYNE [*coldly*] I beg your pardon?

SWINDON. I cant believe it! What will History say?

BURGOYNE. History, sir, will tell lies, as usual. Come: we must send the safe-conduct. [*He goes out*].

SWINDON [*following distractedly*] My God, my God! We shall be wiped out.

As noon approaches there is excitement in the market place. The gallows which hang there permanently for the terror of evildoers, with such minor advertizers and examples of crime as the pillory, the whipping post, and the stocks, has a new rope attached, with the noose hitched up to one of the uprights, out of reach of the boys. Its ladder, too, has been brought out and placed in position by the town beadle, who stands by to guard it from unauthorized climbing. The Webster-bridge townsfolk are present in force, and in high spirits; for the news has spread that it is the devil's disciple and not the minister that King George and his terrible general are about to hang: consequently the execution can be enjoyed without any misgiving as to its righteousness, or to the cowardice of allowing it to take place without a struggle. There is even some fear of a disappointment as midday approaches and the arrival of the beadle with the ladder remains the only sign of preparation. But at last reassuring shouts of Here they come: Here they are, are heard; and a company of soldiers with fixed bayonets, half British infantry, half Hessians, tramp quickly into the middle of the market place, driving the crowd to the sides.

THE SERGEANT. Halt, Front. Dress. [*The soldiers change their column into a square enclosing the gallows, their petty officers, energetically led by the sergeant, hustling the persons who find themselves inside the square out at the corners*]. Now then! Out of it with you: out of it. Some o youll get strung up yourselves presently. Form that square there, will you, you damned Hoosians. No use talkin German to them: talk to their toes with the butt ends of your muskets: theyll understand that. Get out of it, will you. [*He comes upon Judith, standing near the gallows*]. Now then: youve no call here.

JUDITH. May I not stay? What harm am I doing?

SERGEANT. I want none of your argufying. You ought to be ashamed of yourself, running to see a man hanged thats not your husband. And he's no better than yourself. I told my major he was a gentleman; and then he goes and tries to strangle him, and calls his blessed Majesty a lunatic. So out of it with you, double quick.

JUDITH. Will you take these two silver dollars and let me stay?

The sergeant, without an instant's hesitation, looks quickly and furtively round as he shoots the money dexterously into his pocket. Then he raises his voice in virtuous indignation.

THE SERGEANT. Me take money in the execution of my duty! Certainly not. Now I'll tell you what I'll do, to teach you to corrupt the King's officer. I'll put you under arrest until the execution's over. You just stand there; and dont let me see you as much as move from that spot until youre let. [*With a swift wink at her he points to the corner of the square behind the gallows on his right, and turns noisily away, shouting*] Now then, dress up and keep em back, will you.

Cries of Hush and Silence are heard among the townsfolk; and the sound of a military band, playing the Dead March from Saul, is heard. The crowd becomes quiet at once; and the sergeant and petty officers, hurrying to the back of the square, with a few whispered orders and some stealthy hustling cause it to open and admit the funeral procession, which is protected from the crowd by a double file of soldiers. First come Burgoyne and Swindon, who, on entering the square, glance with distaste at the gallows, and avoid passing under it by wheeling a little to the right and stationing themselves on that side. Then Mr Brudenell, the chaplain, in his surplice, with his prayer book open in his hand, walking beside Richard, who is moody and disorderly. He walks doggedly through the gallows framework, and posts himself a little in front of it. Behind him comes the executioner, a stalwart soldier in his shirtsleeves. Following him, two soldiers haul a light military waggon. Finally comes the band, which posts itself at the back of the square, and finishes the Dead March. Judith, watching Richard, painfully steals down to the gallows, and stands leaning against its right post. During the conversation which follows, the two soldiers place the cart under the gallows, and stand by the shafts, which point backwards. The executioner takes a set of steps from the cart and places it ready for the prisoner to mount. Then he climbs the tall ladder which stands against the gallows, and cuts the string by which the rope is hitched up; so that the noose drops dangling over the cart, into which he steps as he descends.

RICHARD [*with suppressed impatience to Brudenell*] Look here, sir: this is no place for a man of your profession. Hadnt you better go away?

SWINDON. I appeal to you, prisoner, if you have any sense of decency left, to listen to the ministrations of the chaplain, and pay due heed to the solemnity of the occasion.

THE CHAPLAIN [*gently reproving Richard*] Try to control yourself, and submit to the divine will. [*He lifts his book to proceed with the service*].

RICHARD. Answer for your own will, sir, and those of your accomplices here [*indicating Burgoyne and Swindon*]: I see little divinity about them or you. You talk to me of Christianity when you are in the act of hanging your enemies. Was there ever such blasphemous nonsense! [*To Swindon, more rudely*] Youve got up the solemnity of the occasion, as you call it, to impress the people with your own dignity—Handel's music and a clergyman to make murder look like piety! Do you suppose *I* am going to help you? Youve asked me to choose the rope because you dont know your own trade well enough to shoot me properly. Well, hang away and have done with it.

SWINDON [*to the chaplain*] Can you do nothing with him, Mr Brudenell?

CHAPLAIN. I will try, sir. [*Beginning to read*] Man that is born of woman hath—

RICHARD [*fixing his eyes on him*] "Thou shalt not kill."

The book drops in Brudenell's hands.

CHAPLAIN [*confessing his embarrassment*] What am I to say, Mr Dudgeon?

RICHARD. Let me alone, cant you?

BURGOYNE [*with extreme urbanity*] I think, Mr Brudenell, that as the usual professional observations seem to strike Mr Dudgeon as

90

incongruous under the circumstances, you had better omit them until—er—until Mr Dudgeon can no longer be inconvenienced by them. [*Brudenell, with a shrug, shuts his book and retires behind the gallows*]. You seem in a hurry, Mr Dudgeon.

RICHARD [*with the horror of death upon him*] Do you think this is a pleasant sort of thing to be kept waiting for? Youve made up your mind to commit murder: well, do it and have done with it.

BURGOYNE. Mr Dudgeon: we are only doing this—

RICHARD. Because youre paid to do it.

SWINDON. You insolent— [*he swallows his rage*].

BURGOYNE [*with much charm of manner*] Ah, I am really sorry that you should think that, Mr Dudgeon. If you knew what my commission cost me, and what my pay is, you would think better of me. I should be glad to part from you on friendly terms.

RICHARD. Hark ye, General Burgoyne. If you think that I like being hanged, youre mistaken. I dont like it; and I dont mean to pretend that I do. And if you think I'm obliged to you for hanging me in a gentlemanly way, youre wrong there too. I take the whole business in devilish bad part; and the only satisfaction I have in it is that youll feel a good deal meaner than I'll look when it's over. [*He turns away, and is striding to the cart when Judith advances and interposes with her arms stretched out to him. Richard, feeling that a very little will upset his self-possession, shrinks from her, crying*] What are you doing here? This is no place for you. [*She makes a gesture as if to touch him. He recoils impatiently*] No: go away, go away: youll unnerve me. Take her away, will you.

JUDITH. Wont you bid me goodbye?

RICHARD [*allowing her to take his hand*] Oh goodbye, goodbye. Now go—go—quickly. [*She clings to his hand—will not be put off with so cold a last farewell—at last, as he tries to disengage himself, throws herself on his breast in agony*].

SWINDON [*angrily to the sergeant, who, alarmed at Judith's movement, has come from the back of the square to pull her back, and stopped irresolutely on finding that he is too late*] How is this? Why is she inside the lines?

91

SERGEANT [*guiltily*] I dunno, sir. She's that artful—cant keep her away.

BURGOYNE. You were bribed.

SERGEANT [*protesting*] No, sir—

SWINDON [*severely*] Fall back. [*He obeys*].

RICHARD [*imploringly to those around him, and finally to Burgoyne, as the least stolid of them*] Take her away. Do you think I want a woman near me now?

BURGOYNE [*going to Judith and taking her hand*] Here, madam: you had better keep inside the lines; but stand here behind us; and dont look.

Richard, with a great sobbing sigh of relief as she releases him and turns to Burgoyne, flies for refuge to the cart and mounts into it. The executioner takes off his coat and pinions him.

JUDITH [*resisting Burgoyne quietly and drawing her hand away*] No: I must stay. I wont look. [*She goes to the right of the gallows. She tries to look at Richard, but turns away with a frightful shudder, and falls on her knees in prayer. Brudenell comes towards her from the back of the square*].

BURGOYNE [*nodding approvingly as she kneels*] Ah, quite so. Do not disturb her, Mr Brudenell: that will do very nicely. [*Brudenell nods also, and withdraws a little, watching her sympathetically. Burgoyne resumes his former position, and takes out a handsome gold chronometer*]. Now then, are those preparations made? We must not detain Mr Dudgeon.

By this time Richard's hands are bound behind him; and the noose is round his neck. The two soldiers take the shafts of the waggon, ready to pull it away. The executioner, standing in the cart behind Richard, makes a sign to the sergeant.

SERGEANT [*to Burgoyne*] Ready, sir.

BURGOYNE. Have you anything more to say, Mr Dudgeon? It wants two minutes of twelve still.

RICHARD [*in a strong voice of a man who has conquered the bitterness of death*] Your watch is two minutes slow by the town clock, which I can see from here, General. [*The town clock strikes the first stroke of twelve. Involuntarily the people flinch at the sound, and a subdued groan breaks from them].* Amen! my life for the world's future!

ANDERSON [*shouting as he rushes into the market place*] Amen; and stop the execution. [*He bursts through the line of soldiers opposite Burgoyne, and rushes, panting, to the gallows*]. I am Anthony Anderson, the man you want.

The crowd, intensely excited, listens with all its ears. Judith, half rising, stares at him; then lifts her hands like one whose dearest prayer has been granted.

SWINDON. Indeed. Then you are just in time to take your place on the gallows. Arrest him.

At a sign from the sergeant, two soldiers come forward to seize Anderson.

ANDERSON [*thrusting a paper under Swindon's nose*] Theres my safe-conduct, sir.

SWINDON [*taken aback*] Safe-conduct! Are you—!

ANDERSON [*emphatically*] I am. [*The two soldiers take him by the elbows*]. Tell these men to take their hands off me.

SWINDON [*to the men*] Let him go.

SERGEANT. Fall back.

The two men return to their places. The townsfolk raise a cheer; and begin to exchange exultant looks, with a presentiment of triumph as they see their Pastor speaking with their enemies in the gate.

ANDERSON [*exhaling a deep breath of relief, and dabbing his perspiring brow with his handkerchief*] Thank God, I was in time!

BURGOYNE [*calm as ever, and still watch in hand*] Ample time, sir. Plenty of time. I should never dream of hanging any gentleman by an American clock. [*He puts up his watch*].

ANDERSON. Yes: we are some minutes ahead of you already, General. Now tell them to take the rope from the neck of that American citizen.

BURGOYNE [*to the executioner in the cart—very politely*] Kindly undo Mr Dudgeon.

The executioner takes the rope from Richard's neck, unties his hands, and helps him on with his coat.

JUDITH [*stealing timidly to Anderson*] Tony.

ANDERSON [*putting his arm round her shoulders and bantering her affectionately*] Well, what do you think of your husband now, eh?—eh??—eh???

JUDITH. I am ashamed—[*she hides her face against his breast*].

BURGOYNE [*to Swindon*] You look disappointed, Major Swindon.

SWINDON. You look defeated, General Burgoyne.

BURGOYNE. I am, sir; and I am humane enough to be glad of it. [*Richard jumps down from the cart, Brudenell offering his hand to help him, and runs to Anderson, whose left hand he shakes heartily, the right being occupied by Judith*]. By the way, Mr Anderson, I do not quite understand. The safe-conduct was for a commander of the militia. I understand you are a—[*He looks as pointedly as his good manners permit at the riding boots, the pistols, and Richard's coat, and adds*]—a clergyman.

ANDERSON [*between Judith and Richard*] Sir; it is in the hour of trial that a man finds his true profession. This foolish young man [*placing his hand on Richard's shoulder*] boasted himself the Devil's Disciple; but when the hour of trial came to him, he found that it was his destiny to suffer and be faithful to the death. I thought myself a decent minister of the gospel of peace; but when the hour of trial came to me, I found that it was my destiny to be a man of action, and that my place was amid the thunder of the captains and the shouting. So I am starting life at fifty as Captain Anthony Anderson of the Springtown militia; and the Devil's Disciple here will start presently as the Reverend Richard Dudgeon, and wag his pow in my old pulpit, and give good advice to this silly sentimental little wife of mine [*putting his other hand on her shoulder. She steals a glance at Richard to see how the prospect pleases him*]. Your mother told me, Richard, that I should never have chosen Judith if I'd been born for the ministry. I am afraid she was right; so, by your leave, you may keep my coat and I'll keep yours.

94

☞ Anderson changes to make himself more interesting for Judith.

RICHARD. Minister—I should say Captain. I have behaved like a fool.

JUDITH. Like a hero.

RICHARD. Much the same thing, perhaps. [*With some bitterness towards himself*] But no: if I had been any good, I should have done for you what you did for me, instead of making a vain sacrifice.

ANDERSON. Not vain, my boy. It takes all sorts to make a world —saints as well as soldiers. [*Turning to Burgoyne*] And now, General, time presses; and America is in a hurry. Have you realized that though you may occupy towns and win battles, you cannot conquer a nation?

BURGOYNE. My good sir, without a Conquest you cannot have an aristocracy. Come and settle the matter at my quarters.

ANDERSON. At your service, sir. [*To Richard*] See Judith home for me, will you, my boy. [*He hands her over to him*]. Now, General. [*He goes busily up the market place towards the Town Hall, leaving Judith and Richard together. Burgoyne follows him a step or two; then checks himself and turns to Richard*].

BURGOYNE. Oh, by the way, Mr Dudgeon, I shall be glad to see you at lunch at half-past one. [*He pauses a moment and adds, with politely veiled slyness*] Bring Mrs Anderson, if she will be so good. [*To Swindon, who is fuming*] Take it quietly, Major Swindon: your friend the British soldier can stand up to anything except the British War Office. [*He follows Anderson*].

SERGEANT [*to Swindon*] What orders, sir?

SWINDON [*savagely*] Orders! What use are orders now! Theres no army. Back to quarters; and be d— [*He turns on his heel and goes*].

SERGEANT [*pugnacious and patriotic, repudiating the idea of defeat*] 'Tention. Now then: cock up your chins, and shew em you dont care a damn for em. Slope arms! Fours! Wheel! Quick march!

The drums mark time with a tremendous bang; the band strikes up British Grenadiers; and the Sergeant, Brudenell, and the English troops march off defiantly to their quarters. The townsfolk press in behind, and follow them up the market, jeering at them; and the town band, a very primitive affair, brings up the rear, playing Yankee Doodle. Essie, who comes in with them, runs to Richard.

ESSIE. Oh, Dick!

RICHARD [*good-humoredly, but wilfully*] Now, now: come, come! I dont mind being hanged: but I will not be cried over.

ESSIE. No, I promise. I'll be good. [*She tries to restrain her tears, but cannot*]. I—I want to see where the soldiers are going to. [*She goes a little way up the market, pretending to look after the crowd*].

JUDITH. Promise me you will never tell him.

RICHARD. Dont be afraid.

They shake hands on it.

ESSIE [*calling to them*] Theyre coming back. They want you.

Jubilation in the market. The townsfolk surge back again in wild enthusiasm with their band, and hoist Richard on their shoulders, cheering him.

Glossary: reading the text

Preface

1 *Alpinist*   mountain climber.

   toilsome   involving hard work.

2 *inane*   empty.

   drab   keep company with prostitutes.

   metropolitan   of London.

   sedentary employment   here referring to clerks, office workers etc.

   sporting publican   here meaning wealthy innkeeper who enjoys horse racing and boxing.

3 *Jejunely insipid*   unsatisfying and tasteless.

   masquerade   false show, pretence.

   clandestine   secret.

   licentiousness   lewdness.

4 *guinea ... shilling*   old British currency (20 shillings to a pound, 21 in a guinea).

   caprice   unpredictable change of mind.

   wiseacres   people who follow fashions and crazes.

5 *Strafford, Colombe's Birthday, The Cenci*   plays by Browning and Shelley (English poets).

   faddists   people who follow fashions and crazes.

   Ibsen   Norwegian dramatist (1828–1906) whose plays such as **A Doll's House** and **Ghosts** dealt with moral and social issues.

   Maeterlinck   (1862–1949) Belgian dramatist.

   epithet   here, term of abuse.

actor-managers   leading actors often formed their own companies and produced plays themselves.

Sir Henry Irving   (1838–1905) great English actor – the first to be knighted.

Miss Ellen Terry   (1847–1928) leading English actress, partner of Irving. Shaw was infatuated with her and wrote parts for her.

Abbots of Misrule   these presided over the revels in a nobleman's house.

6 **vapid**   flat.

more Rebecca and less Rowena   more Jewish characters than Christian.

Justice Shallow   Shakespearean character (**Henry IV, Part 2**).

bona roba   showy lewd woman.

7 **Pharisaical**   self-righteous person (from New Testament references to the Jewish sect, Pharisees).

8 **Pasha**   Turkish governor.

Mrs Warren's   Mrs Warren was a successful brothel keeper.

9 **Bohemianism**   socially unconventional.

Tom Robertson   English dramatist (1829–71).

Board of Guardians   board which administered the system of poor relief.

Hedda Gabler   feminist heroine of Ibsen's play by the same name.

10 **Mrs Tanqueray   The Second Mrs Tanqueray** is a play by the English dramatist Sir Arthur Pinero (1855–1934).

Saint Teresa   Spanish saint (1515–82) who led a life of extreme asceticism.

11 **poesy**   archaic word for poetry.

odalisque   Eastern female slave.

cadi   judge in Muslim country.

12 **corporealities**   bodily matter.

Martin Luther   German religious reformer (1483–1546).

H. G. Wells   English writer (1866–1946).

Bostonian Utopia   an ideal society, set (fictionally) in the USA.

13 *Fourier*   Charles Fourier (1772–1837), French social theorist who advocated a form of collective society.

Owen   Robert Owen (1771–1858), Welsh social reformer who had similar ideas to Fourier.

millennial   believing they had created a perfect society.

Paolo and Francesca   characters in Dante's *Inferno*.

scout   (here) reject with scorn.

Lamarckian   from the theory of evolution proposed by Jean Lamarck (1744–1829).

14 *Kaisers*   German emperors.

Puritans   those who are strict in the practice of religion or morality; opposed to frivolous pleasure.

Milton   John Milton (1608–74), English poet; a noted Puritan.

Cromwell   Oliver Cromwell (1599–1658), Puritan leader of the Parliamentary opposition to King Charles I; later Protector during the Commonwealth (1649–58).

Bunyan   John Bunyan (1628–88), English writer, author of *Pilgrim's Progress*.

voluptuaries   lovers of pleasure.

15 *Flogging Bills*   Bills to restore punishment by flogging.

androgynous   neither male nor female.

Philistine   uncultured.

Platonic   confined to words or theory.

Bismarckian   like Bismarck, the powerful German statesman (1815–98).

illude   deceive.

Cervantes   (1547–1616) Spanish author of *Don Quixote*.

16 *vainglorious*   extremely vain.

Quintessence   absolute essence.

Ingrates   ungrateful people.

Schopenhauer   German philosopher (1788–1860).

cart in Hyde Park   probably near Speakers' Corner where crowds gathered to hear political and religious speakers orating from numbered wagons on a nearby park roadway.

mountebank   charlatan.

motley   incongruous mixture.

17 *beglamored*   dazzled.

18 *trumpet and cartwheel*   rather like the travelling salesmen who stood on carts to proclaim their wares.

Flying Dutchman   doomed to travel the world until redeemed by love.

claptraps   language used to gain applause.

Buckstone's Wreck Ashore   This melodrama by J B Buckstone (1802–79) was one of the most popular melodramas of the nineteenth century, with three major productions at the Adelphi (the theatre for which Shaw wrote *The Devil's Disciple*) between 1830 and 1880.

19 *Covenanter*   the Scottish Covenanters swore an oath to defend Presbyterianism.

Diabolonian   of the devil.

Prometheus   demigod who stole fire from the gods and gave it to man.

Wagnerian Siegfried   Siegfried is the hero of the *Ring* cycle of four operas by Richard Wagner (1813–83).

William Blake   English poet and painter (1757–1827).

20 *plagiarist*   one who copies ideas or work from others.

Nietzsche   German philosopher (1844–1900).

metaphysic   philosophy.

21 *penny-in-the-slot heroes*   heroes who are like the automata in fairground machines.

Act I

23 *New Hampshire*   state in New England, USA, which declared itself independent from Britain in 1776.

Websterbridge   fictional town.

prepossessing woman   attractive.

barren forms ... dead Puritanism   Shaw here implies that Puritanism, which inspired the early English settlers, had by now become stale.

pen   shut in.

felony   crime.

licentious   disregarding accepted morality.

seventh commandment   from the Bible: 'Thou shalt not commit adultery'.

Presbyterian   The Presbyterian Church is strong in Scotland and Northern Ireland, and had a large membership in the American colonies. It is based on the teachings of John Calvin (1509–64), who proclaimed that salvation was through faith, not by good works alone. The church is run by councils comprising elders, lay members of the congregations, and the clergy.

Rights of Man   a book by Tom Paine (1737–1809), who championed republicanism, and borrowed the title of the book from the French Declaration of the Rights of Man, 1789, after the date when the play's events take place.

24 *fender*   fire guard.

laths   strips.

domestic altar of the fireplace   ironical religious reference.

sconce   candle holder.

scullery   room for washing dishes etc.

dwarf dresser   small sideboard with shelves.

stridulous   harsh.

rent   torn.

25 *rudely*   roughly.

cowed   subdued.

Christy   short for Christopher.

plaid   with a chequered or tartan pattern.

peremptorily   admitting no refusal.

26 *phlegmatically*   coolly, calmly.

stupent   struck with amazement.

Nevinstown   fictional town.

27 *bovine*   like an ox.

railing   speaking abusively.

divine   clergyman.

secular   not religious.

conciliatory   bringing together those who disagree.

sanguine   blood-red; a sanguine humour denoted courage and optimism.

28 *recalcitrant*   obstinately disobedient.

Springtown   fictional town.

I must bear my cross   a saying which means to suffer like Christ on the way to his crucifixion.

vindictively   seeking revenge.

dissolute   lacking morals, especially with regard to sex.

29 *prodigal son*   from the biblical parable; the son wasted his life and money in dissolute living, but was welcomed home by his father when he repented of this life.

We are told ... punished   there are many references to this in the Bible (e.g. Isaiah 13:11).

30 *marriage portion*   dowry.

   told that the heart ... things   biblical quotation (Jeremiah 17:9).

   latchet   buckle; biblical reference to the words spoken by John the Baptist, not feeling himself worthy to loose the latchet on Christ's shoes.

32 *decanter*   glass bottle for holding wine or spirits.

   state occasion   ironic reference to a family gathering such as a funeral or christening.

   green ware   type of crockery for everyday use.

   barnbrack   a teacake with currants in it.

   snuff   the burnt part of the wick.

33 *patronizingly*   in a superior manner.

   complacent amiability   in a self-satisfied and pleasant manner.

34 *edified*   improved morally.

   condescension   kindliness to inferior person.

35 *ostentatiously shocked*   aiming to be obviously noticed.

   wrestles ... Sunday   such activities were thought of as sinful by Puritans.

36 *allowed precedence*   allowed to enter first.

   learned professions   (here) the Law and the Church.

   bottle-nosed   with a red nose through drinking too much alcohol.

   no ascetic   not someone who practises severe self-discipline.

   derelict   abandoned.

   callousness   insensitivity.

   reprobate   sinner.

37 *We are all ... Throne*   we are all equal in the sight of God.

38 *sardonic*   scornful.

   satirical   (here) sarcastic.

   picturesquely careless   dressed probably deliberately in a casual manner in order to appear unconventional.

upright horsedealer   horsedealers had a reputation for dishonesty; the adjective is thus intended sarcastically.

overborne   overcome.

39 **unction**   fervent quality in words caused by religious emotion (from anointing with oil).

40 **wrath**   anger; often used in Bible.

checkmated   defeated, as in chess.

41 **consolations of the law**   the usual phrase is 'without the consolations of religion', i.e. to die an unbeliever or not to receive the last rites.

For what we are about ...   the start of a prayer before a meal.

annuity   pension.

42 **'And I recommend her ...'**   the whole sentence shows that Timothy was being ironic.

The fatted calf   killed by the prodigal son's father to provide a feast when the son came home (see note to page 29).

43 **cock of the walk**   the dominant person.

weight of the law on women   at this time, women had few rights to own property.

Mary Wollstonecraft   feminist writer (1759–97); author of **A Vindication of the rights of Woman** (1792) and mother of Mary Shelley.

44 **cleaving to**   sticking to.

draught   drink.

45 **Devil was my natural master ...**   see Preface, pages 19–20.

Major Swindon   a fictional British officer.

46 **King George**   King George III (1738–1820); here meaning the British Government.

dancing on nothing   the twitching of a hanged man.

> 1 Which actions of Dick show him behaving like a melodramatic hero? Which of his comments reinforce this impression?
>
> 2 What do we learn about Essie?
>
> 3 Why does Dick offer her protection at the end of the Act?

Act 2

47 *griddle*   circular iron plate for baking.

American cloth   oilcloth, with a treated waterproof surface.

chapped   roughened.

japanned   varnished, usually in black.

trencher   wooden plate or dish for serving food.

oak press   large oak cupboard with shelves for clothes etc.

48 *drugget*   rough fabric floor-covering.

mezzotint   a type of engraved print.

Raphael   Italian painter (1483–1520).

rococo   highly ornamented style of decoration prevalent in eighteenth-century Europe.

cowrie   type of shell.

Mr Philip Webb   an English architect (1831–1915) who, with others such as Edwin Lutyens, promoted a style known as English Vernacular, based on rural domestic architecture of the seventeenth century.

49 *King George*   (here) British troops.

50 *what death must mean for a man like that*   as a sinner, Dudgeon would go to hell.

51 *tax*   make demands upon.

52 *stands on much ceremony*   insists on formalities.

cynically   disbelieving of human goodness.

53 *break bread*   have a meal; biblical reference to the Last Supper which Christ had with his disciples.

54 *If all my enemies ...*   this refers to the Christian maxim: 'love your enemies'.

58 *man of my cloth*   a clergyman is often referred to as a 'man of the cloth'; note also that by putting on the coat, Dick has 'become' a clergyman.

59 *game one*   a spirited one.

ought to a bin   ought to have been.

Muffle the drums   drums are muffled for a funeral march.

65 *choleric*   irascible, angry.

66 *dying to save you*   as Christ died to save others.

Blood an' owns!   a soldier's oath: by Christ's blood and wounds.

---

1   What sort of a marriage do you think the Andersons have?

2   Why doesn't Judith want Dick to leave the house?

3   What clues are we given before the soldiers arrive that they will mistake him for the clergyman?

Act 3

68 *mum*   madam (ma'am).

kep   kept.

Bridewell   prison; the original Bridewell was in London.

court martial   military trial.

slep   slept.

spoil five   game in which the deal is spoilt if no player takes three of the five tricks.

raffish   rakish, flashy.

69 *General Burgoyne*   British general (1722–92) who commanded one of the British armies in the War of Independence.

Portugal   Burgoyne captured Valencia de Alcantara in Portugal during the Seven Years' War.

on the wing   in flight.

70 *changing clothes with me*   there are many stories of prisoners escaping by changing clothes with those of a female visitor.

cow   subdue.

only man I have any right to kill   technically true, but suicide is a sin in Christianity.

71 *divining the truth*   realising the truth (that Judith is in love with him).

73 *G.R.*   Georgius Rex (Latin for King George).

elopement   running away (from parents etc.) to get married.

fastidiousness   tendency to be easily disgusted.

74 *profane language*   swearing.

75 *Hessians, Brunswickers . . .*   the British army employed mercenaries from the German states (George III was also Elector of Hanover).

dragoon   cavalry soldier.

dissenter   member of a sect which has separated itself from the Established Church.

76 *sit at the feet of Gamaliel*   biblical reference to Gamaliel, a highly reputed doctor of law.

77 *soldier to think*   soldiers are expected to obey orders.

78 *hanged for a sheep . . . lamb*   might as well be hanged for a large offence as a small one.

79 *Lord North's robbing me*   Lord North (1732–92) was Prime Minister from 1770 to 1782. His insistence on taxing the American colonists despite the fact they were not represented in Parliament led to the War of Independence.

stamp duty . . . tea duty   two of the most resented taxes.

pig-headed lunatic   George III did in fact become insane, but not until 1788, after the time of this play.

stentorian   with a powerful voice.

80 leave you to the provo-marshal's pistol   leave you to be finished off by a shot from the provost marshal, the head of the military police.

black cap   worn by judges as they pronounce the death sentence.

82 blatant   (here) conspicuous, unashamed.

83 zany   clown.

He's the bad brother...   a common device in melodrama was to have two brothers – one good, one bad.

85 understrapper   underling.

87 adjutant   assistant to superior officer.

Quebec... New York... Albany   in 1777 Burgoyne marched from Canada to try to isolate New England.

Jobbery   corruption; using a public position for private gain.

Red Tape   excessive use of formality or regulations in public affairs.

Saratoga   Burgoyne surrendered at Saratoga to General Gates on 17 October 1777.

88 pillory ... stocks   old forms of punishment in which offenders were held in wooden frames and exposed to public ridicule and missiles.

Dress   line up in ranks.

argufying   slang for arguing.

89 dress up   line up.

Dead March from Saul   a tune from an oratorio by Handel (1685–1759), often used in grand funerals.

surplice   long white robe worn over a black cassock by clergy when conducting a service.

90 Man that is born of woman ...   the start of the burial service in the Church of England's **Book of Common Prayer**.

'Thou shalt not kill'   one of the Ten Commandments, from the Bible.

urbanity   polished manners.

91 **incongruous**   out of place.

what my commission cost me   until the nineteenth century, most men had to buy their commissions as officers.

92 **stolid**   unemotional.

pinions   ties his arms behind his back.

chronometer   watch.

93 **their enemies in the gate**   biblical phrase.

94 **suffer and be faithful to the death**   from the **Book of Common Prayer**.

thunder of the captains   biblical phrase for battle.

wag his pow   shake his head (Scottish).

95 **Conquest**   the English aristocracy claimed superiority if they could trace their ancestry to the Norman Conquest (1066).

British Grenadiers   famous regimental march.

96 **Yankee Doodle**   adopted as a march by the New Englanders.

1	In what ways have Dick's behaviour and demeanour changed?
2	What can you deduce about the character of General Burgoyne?
3	What role does Major Swindon play? In what ways is he a contrast to General Burgoyne?

Study programme

Characters

1 Write detailed notes on each of the characters in the play. Make it clear how much we are told about each person by:

- other people;
- Shaw himself in his stage directions, and therefore, by what that character actually does and the way in which he/she says things. (Shaw is very clear about the way in which certain lines should be spoken.)

2 What do you think Dick will do in his life following his release? Write this up as a magazine article, complete with eye-catching headline, using word-processed format if possible.

3 Imagine that, as General Burgoyne, you have to write a report to your superiors in London on the incidents in Act 3. Make notes before you attempt your first draft.

4 Why does Judith Anderson move from an apparent loathing of Dick to falling in love with him? What clues are we given in the play to her change of attitude?

5 Do you think Dick will keep his promise to Judith not to tell her husband about her feelings for him? Will Judith tell her husband?

Discuss these questions in pairs; then write up your views. Justify your answers, using clues to the characters provided in the play.

6 Why do you think Mrs Dudgeon is portrayed as a bitter woman? What has happened to her to make her so?

7 Why are we told that Essie is only about 16 or 17? How does this affect her possible relationship with Dick?

8 Write a scene showing what had happened before the play opens; for example, the death of Timothy Dudgeon or the hanging of Peter Dudgeon at which Dick was present.

9 On page 55, Dick says: 'He wrung my heart by being a man. Need you tear it by being a woman?' What is Dick's attitude to women?

10 Why do you think Dick rejects his mother so decisively?

11 Is Dick a fool or a hero? Debate this question in small groups.

Dramatic technique

1 How does Shaw employ the techniques of melodrama in the course of the play? Find as many instances as you can. The Introduction (pages x–xiv) is worth rereading here.

2 RICHARD ... I do not interfere with your sermons; do not you interrupt mine.

Act I, page 44

Why does Shaw apparently warn us of something dull coming up? What in fact happens next? Find other examples in the play of Shaw using this technique.

3 There are many references to time in the play, although the action takes place over only two days. Make a list of these references. Then write an essay on how Shaw uses them to increase the dramatic tension.

4 How does Shaw use the colours and styles of the characters' clothes to enhance the drama? Consider particularly the part played by the clergyman's coat.

5 The action of the play moves from a domestic interior to public spaces, culminating in a large exterior space. How does the change in Dick's role and attitude mirror these changes?

6 How does Shaw use music in the play? What purpose does it serve?

In performance

1 Design a theatre programme for a production of **The Devil's Disciple**. You will need to think about:

- a cover (which will double as a poster);
- notes on the author;
- notes on the plot to whet the audience's appetite;
- cast lists;
- brief notes on the characters and the actors who will be playing them.

Present your programme as a booklet, complete with art work.

2 You have been asked by a major TV company to submit your proposals for a TV version of **The Devil's Disciple**. They want you to concentrate on the scene of the reading of the will.

In order to win the contract, you must prepare the following.

- Costume design.
- Casting. Who will you want to see in the roles? Why are they suitable? Will they help to attract an audience and thus make the play successful? What acting work have they done before which makes you think they are a good choice?

- Music. You will need to suggest title music and any incidental music.
- Stage directions. You have to provide any additional camera movements, close-ups and so on.

In pairs or small groups, draft out your ideas. Then write up your proposals.

3 As an alternative to the previous suggestion, provide a story-board for a TV version. This involves drawing a series of cartoons representing the way the camera would show the scenes. You should work on a storyboard presentation of a complete Act.

4 You have been asked to direct a performance for an amateur drama company. They have little money and you have to stage it with a minimum of props and scenery. How would you achieve this, remaining as true to the story as possible?

5 It has often been pointed out that there is a flaw in the last Act. There seems to be no reason not to continue with the hanging, given that the British know Dick's real identity already, and given that they cannot substitute Anderson, with his safe-conduct pass.

Rewrite this part of the last Act, either giving more convincing reasons for Dick's release, or leading to his hanging and subsequent events.

6 The action of the play is advanced by many off-stage events. Write one of these scenes as a play, and act it out in groups. Use a cassette/video to record your performance.

7 Read the following two reviews of the 1994 National Theatre production at the Olivier Theatre, London. What do the critics see as the strengths and weaknesses of the play itself? Do you agree?

Which theatrical moments in **The Devil's Disciple** catch these reviewers' attention?

A flightless Superman

... *mild diversion is what* The Devil's Disciple *now amounts to. Taking the standard ingredients of Victorian melodrama, from the Reading of the Will to the Gallows Reprieve, it at once parades and relentlessly, impudentlypunctures them. Sometimes, though, this merely results in one distorting extreme being replaced by another. The typical melodramatic hero is motivated to self-sacrifice exclusively by romantic love. Shaw programmatically reverses this in the figure of Dick Dudgeon, the trainee Shavian 'Superman' who is prepared, 'with no motive and no interest' and no tendresse for the minister's wife, to be arrested and sent to the gallows in mistake for him.*

There could be something worryingly inhuman, rather than superhuman, about such impersonal goodness. Happily, Richard Bonneville, who brings a fine subversive panache to the part, also throws out suggestions that Dick's militant anti-romantic stance is that of a romantic who's leaning over backwards not to be. His performance adds further humanising touches like the shuddering fit of delayed shock he allows himself shortly after his release from the gallows.

The show is traditionally stolen in the last act by the arrival of Burgoyne, the urbane English general with a shrewd understanding of the perils of Anglo-Saxon gentlemanliness. Mindful of this, perhaps, a fine Daniel Massey camps up the arch-suavity of the man; to the point where you feel he might actually break out into a Jack Buchanan-style song and dance. He's splendidly supported by Jeremy Sinden's hilarious study of porcine pomposity as Major Swindon.

From the scrubbed virtue and stirred-up emotionalism of Helen McCrory's Judith to Frances Cuka's grim, black-bonneted battleaxe of a mother, the parts are vividly registered. But this is not a production which colonises the Olivier with any great convictions. A large map of New England and a weak two-dimensional cluster of clapboard houses endeavour to fill up a space which only comes into its own in the gallows scene. The other problem is the play, whose staled subversiveness now comes lukewarm off the grid.

Paul Taylor, **Independent**, 10 September 1994

Good for nothing

Borges once said that Shaw's work leaves one with a flavour of liberation. That hit home this week while watching two excellent productions: Christopher Morahan's The Devil's Disciple at the Olivier and Gale Edwards's Saint Joan at the Strand. In both plays we witness the triumph of the protesting conscience over received ideas and political necessity; and, with both plays climaxing in trials, it is fascinating to note how the aristocratic wit of General Burgoyne modulates into the smooth-tongued apologias of Warwick and Joan's Inquisitor.

The Devil's Disciple *is obviously the lighter play: an inversion of standard Victorian melodrama set during the American war of independence. And the case against it can be simply stated. Dick Dudgeon, the eponymous hero ready to take the place on the gallows of a rebel parson, lacks any hint of real diabolism. And the dialogue of the first two acts could have been written by almost anybody: plot mechanics supersede intellectual exploration.*

But, if the play gives off that heady quality of liberation Borges spoke of, it is entirely due to the glorious third act. Shaw throws melodramatic values to the winds by proposing the idea of motiveless goodness. In conventional melodrama Dudgeon would take the parson's place on the gallows out of love for his wife or political heroism. Here he acts out of a spontaneous feeling and natural virtue which is common in life and almost unknown on the stage. The smart money today is on Shaw as fusty and dated: in fact he creates in Dick Dudgeon one of drama's first existential heroes.

The play's sense of liberation also owes everything to the third-act emergence of General Burgoyne, the sardonic commander of the beleaguered British troops. In theory Shaw was suspicious of the aristocratic temperament capable of justifying hanging on the grounds of political expediency; in reality, Burgoyne runs off with the play partly through his native wit and partly through his Shavian contempt for the bone-headed stupidity of professional soldiers and the negligence of the British War Office. Daniel Massey here plays him to perfection as a man who adopts a pose of ironic languor to disguise his outrage at the 'jobbery and snobbery, incompetence and red tape' that led to the loss of the American colonies.

Admittedly the play creaks a bit in the first two acts. But Morahan and his designer, John Gunter, frame these first two acts in narrow, trucked-on sets as if to evoke the closed-in spirit of New England self-denial. The production opens out, physically and spiritually, in the final act and the performances take off. Richard Bonneville's Dudgeon has a fine moment when, released from the gallows, he sinks to his knees in a spirit of delayed, quivering funk. Paul Jesson's Anthony Anderson, charging down the centre-aisle to ironic cheers, also suggests the intemperate man of action under the clerical cloth. And Helen McCrory does everything possible to redeem the parson's romantically fixated wife. But the acting honours really belong to Massey and to Jeremy Sinden whose Major Swindon embodies, to fruity perfection, the stonewall complacency of the British military mind. It is in the final act, with its ironic reversals and verbal satire, that what CE Montague called Shaw's 'imp of genius' finally appears to achieve the desired liberation.

Michael Billington, **Guardian**, 10 September 1994

Further assignments

☐ *The Devil's Disciple* is a play about:

- the rebellion of a man against his family;
- the willingness of a man to sacrifice himself to save another;
- (a satire on) religion and its effects on people;
- the incompetence of the British in fighting American colonists;
- how easy it is for someone *un*conventional to alarm conventional society;
- how people do not always behave in predictable ways.

Stage a debate in which group members argue for and against the above statements. Use quotations from the text to support your views.

2 It is quite common nowadays for films to be 'novelised'; that is, their screenplays are turned into novels. Take part of the play and turn it into the chapter of a novel. Think carefully about the differences between writing for the stage and the page!

3 Write a report for the **Websterbridge Gazette** of the events of the last Act. As a civilian, you will not have had access to the trial. How will you have obtained any information about this? You will need to research the style of language used in the eighteenth century.

4

I will have nothing to do with schools and colleges at any price: no book of mine shall ever with my consent be that damnable thing, a schoolbook. Let them buy the dollar editions if they want them. By a school edition they mean an edition with notes and prefaces full of material for such questions as 'Give the age of Bernard Shaw's great aunt when he wrote You Never Can Tell *and state the reasons for believing that the inscription on her tombstone at Ballyhooly is incorrect'. The experienced students read the notes and the prefaces and not the plays, and for ever after loathe my very name.*

Dear Mr Shaw, edited by Vivian Elliot

Is Shaw correct? Either:

- write to him explaining why he is wrong and why an edition like this is useful to you;

or

- write a letter to the publishers explaining why you agree with Shaw.

5 In response to a request for an article for a school magazine, Shaw wrote:

There are many school magazines and they all ask me for contributions. Naturally I prefer larger circulations and princely payments. If there is not enough talent in your Fifth to make the magazine readable, the school should be closed and the teaching staff set to hoe turnips.

Dear Mr Shaw, edited by Vivian Elliot

Can you rise to Shaw's challenge? Imagine that you are the drama critic of the school magazine. Write a review of **The Devil's Disciple** (as a script for reading or as performed on stage).

Remember that most of your readers will not have heard of the play, so you will need to explain the plot, the setting and who the characters are.

Study questions

Many of the activities you have already completed will help you to answer the following questions. Before you begin to write, consider these points about essay writing:

- Analyse what the question is asking. Do this by circling key words or phrases and numbering each part.

- Use each part of the question to 'brainstorm' ideas and references to the play which you think are relevant to the answer.

- Decide on the order in which you are going to tackle the parts of the question. It may help you to draw a flow-diagram of the parts so that you can see which aspects of the question are linked.

- Organise your ideas and quotations into sections to fit your flow-diagram. You can do this by placing notes in columns under the various headings.

- Write a first draft of your essay. Do not concern yourself too much with paragraphing and so on; just aim to get your ideas down on paper and do not be too critical of what you write.

- Redraft as many times as you need, ensuring all the time that:
  - each paragraph addresses the question;
  - each paragraph addresses a new part of the question, or at least develops a part;
  - you have an opening and closing paragraph which are clear and linked to the question set;
  - you have checked for spelling and other grammatical errors.

1. Compare and contrast the characters of Dick Dudgeon and Anthony Anderson.

2. Shaw wrote: 'The progressive man goes through life on the same principle, instinctively making for the focus of struggle and resisting the tendency to edge him out into the place of ease'. Does this explain the motive behind Dick's actions?

3. 'The worst sin towards our fellow creatures is not to hate them, but to be indifferent to them; thats the essence of inhumanity' (Anthony Anderson, Act 2, page 51). Do you agree? How is this theme treated in the play?

4. Michael Holroyd has written: 'Shaw created in Dick Dudgeon an embryo superman to do battle for him against the power and idolatry of sex'. In what way is Dick a superman? Do you agree with Holroyd's assessment?

5. Is melodrama the only form in which the play could have been written? How different would it have been as, for example, a comedy?

6. Discuss the role of women in **The Devil's Disciple**.

7. 'Serious drama is perhaps the most formidable social weapon that a modern reformer can wield.' Do you consider **The Devil's Disciple** to be a play which both educates and entertains its audience?

8. Examine Shaw's treatment of religion and religious groups in **The Devil's Disciple**.

9. *... the London critics ... took Mrs Dudgeon at her own valuation as a religious woman because she was detestably disagreeable. And they took Dick as a blackguard on her authority, because he was neither detestable nor disagreeable.*

   Preface, page 20

119

Discuss the critics' view of these two characters.

[10]   Why *did Dick save Anderson? On the stage, it appears, people do things for reasons. Off the stage they dont.*

Preface, page 21

Do you agree with Shaw's analysis?

Suggestions for further reading

Other works by Bernard Shaw

Pygmalion
Shaw's most popular play. Professor Higgins takes Eliza Doolittle, a flower-seller, and attempts to turn her into a lady. The original story for the film *My Fair Lady*.

Arms and the Man
Bluntschli, a mercenary soldier, hides in Raina's bedroom during a retreat. His down-to-earth realism challenges her romantic view of war and of the gallant Sergius, her fiancé. A comedy which challenges conventional views on war and romance.

Saint Joan
Shaw's version of the story of Joan of Arc. Her struggle to convince the French that she has been chosen by God to rid them of their English occupiers, and her subsequent fight against the English, are powerfully told.

Major Barbara
Andrew Undershaft is an arms manufacturer, while his daughter Barbara is in the Salvation Army, and a clash of morals is inevitable.

Androcles and the Lion
Shaw describes this as a Fable Play. Androcles, an early Christian, pulls a thorn out of the paw of a lion in the jungle. When Androcles is thrown before the lions by the Romans, he meets the same lion...

Cashel Byron's Profession

Shaw's most successful novel. Cashel Byron falls in love with Lydia Carew, and needs to hide from her his profession, which is prize-fighting.

Works by other authors

A Tale of Two Cities by Charles Dickens

Set in London and Paris at the time of the French Revolution, this novel tells the story of the struggle to free the aristocrat Darnay from execution. Sidney Carton, an English lawyer, takes his place on the guillotine.

East Lynne by Mrs Henry Wood

A classic melodrama.

The Heiress by General John Burgoyne

This writer's most successful comedy. The language of the eighteenth century is difficult in places.

Paradise Lost by John Milton

A long poetic account of the rebellion of Satan against the rule of God, written by one of the greatest poets, who was a Puritan.

The Madness of George III by Alan Bennett

A modern play which charts the decline into madness of the king against the background of the loss of the American colonies.

Bernard Shaw: A Reassessment by Colin Wilson

A relatively short critical biography of Shaw, full of interesting ideas about Shaw's work.

Bernard Shaw (volume 1) by Michael Holroyd

The most recent and thorough biography of Shaw.

Wider reading assignments

1. Colin Wilson has summarised Shaw's plays as follows: 'The Shaw drama is ultimately the drama of the intelligent man in the world of the less intelligent, and every detail in the play is engineered to bring out the contrast.' How does Shaw 'engineer the contrast' in *The Devil's Disciple* and other plays?

2. Compare and contrast the characters and actions of Dick Dudgeon and Sidney Carton (*The Tale of Two Cities*).

3. Shaw sets several plays in wartime (*The Devil's Disciple, Arms and the Man, Saint Joan* etc.). How does he use the settings to advance his ideas? Could the plays have been set in peacetime?

4. Write a short study on *melodrama* as a genre, with reference to *The Devil's Disciple* and two other plays you've read which contain ingredients of melodrama.

Longman Literature
Series editor: Roy Blatchford

Novels

Jane Austen   *Pride and Prejudice*   0 582 07720 6
Charlotte Brontë   *Jane Eyre*   0 582 07719 2
Emily Brontë   *Wuthering Heights*   0 582 07782 6
Anita Brookner   *Hotel du Lac*   0 582 25406 X
Marjorie Darke   *A Question of Courage*   0 582 25395 0
Charles Dickens   *A Christmas Carol*   0 582 23664 9
            Great Expectations   0 582 07783 4
            Hard Times   0 582 25407 8
            Oliver Twist   0 582 28729 4
George Eliot   *Silas Marner*   0 582 23662 2
Anne Fine   *Flour Babies*   0 582 29259 X
         Goggle Eyes   0 582 29260 3
         Madame Doubtfire   0 582 29261 1
F Scott Fitzgerald   *The Great Gatsby*   0 582 06023 0
            Tender is the Night   0 582 09716 9
Nadine Gordimer   *July's People*   0 582 06011 7
Graham Greene   *The Captain and the Enemy*   0 582 06024 9
Thomas Hardy   *Far from the Madding Crowd*   0 582 07788 5
            The Mayor of Casterbridge   0 582 22586 8
            Tess of the d'Urbervilles   0 582 09715 0
Susan Hill   *The Mist in the Mirror*   0 582 25399 3
Aldous Huxley   *Brave New World*   0 582 06016 8
Robin Jenkins   *The Cone-Gatherers*   0 582 06017 6
Doris Lessing   *The Fifth Child*   0 582 06021 4
Joan Lindsay   *Picnic at Hanging Rock*   0 582 08174 2
Bernard Mac Laverty   *Lamb*   0 582 06557 7
Jan Mark   *The Hillingdon Fox*   0 582 25985 1
Dalene Matthee   *Fiela's Child*   0 582 28732 4
Brian Moore   *Lies of Silence*   0 582 08170 X
Beverley Naidoo   *Chain of Fire*   0 582 25403 5
            Journey to Jo'burg   0 582 25402 7
George Orwell   *Animal Farm*   0 582 06010 9
Alan Paton   *Cry, the Beloved Country*   0 582 07787 7
Ruth Prawer Jhabvala   *Heat and Dust*   0 582 25398 5
Paul Scott   *Staying On*   0 582 07718 4
Virginia Woolf   *To the Lighthouse*   0 582 09714 2

Short stories

Jeffrey Archer   *A Twist in the Tale*   0 582 06022 2
Thomas Hardy   *The Wessex Tales*   0 582 25405 1
Susan Hill   *A Bit of Singing and Dancing*   0 582 09711 8
George Layton   *A Northern Childhood*   0 582 25404 3
Bernard Mac Laverty   *The Bernard Mac Laverty Collection*   0 582 08172 6
Angelou, Goodison, Senior & Walker   *A Quartet of Stories*   0 582 28730 8

Poetry

Five Modern Poets   edited by Barbara Bleiman   0 582 09713 4
Poems from Other Centuries   edited by Adrian Tissier   0 582 22595 X
Poems in my Earphone   collected by John Agard   0 582 22587 6
Poems One   edited by Celeste Flower   0 582 25400 0
Poems Two   edited by Paul Jordan & Julia Markus   0 582 25401 9

Longman Group Limited
Edinburgh Gate, Harlow,
Essex, CM20 2JE
and Associated Companies throughout the world.

This educational edition first published 1995

Editorial material set in 10/12 point Gill Sans Light
Produced by Longman Singapore Publishers (Pte) Ltd,
Printed in Singapore

ISBN 0 582 25410 8
Second impression 1996

Cover illustration by Tony McSweeny

ACKNOWLEDGEMENTS

We are grateful to the following for permission to reproduce
copyright material: The Guardian for the Michael Billington Review
'Good for nothing' in *The Guardian* © 10.9.94; Newspaper Publishing
Plc for the Paul Taylor Review in *The Independent* 10.9.94.

The publisher's policy is to use paper manufactured from sustainable
forests.

Consultants: Geoff Barton and Jackie Head